GW00983837

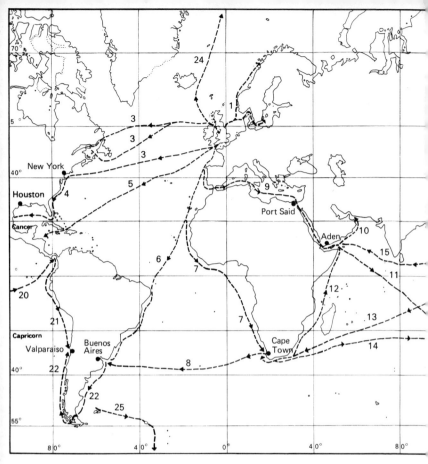

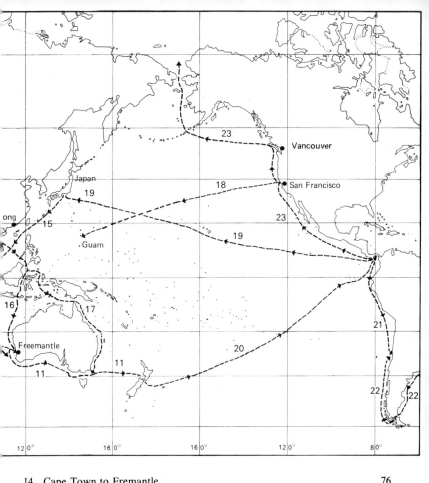

A GUIDE TO

SEABIRDS
ON THE OCEAN ROUTES

A GUIDE TO

SEABIRDS

ON THE OCEAN ROUTES

Captain G. S. Tuck
D.S.O., Royal Navy

Illustrated by
Norman Arlott

COLLINS
Grafton Street, London

William Collins Sons & Co Ltd
London · Glasgow · Sydney · Auckland
Toronto · Johannesburg

First published 1980
Reprinted 1985
© G. S. Tuck 1980
ISBN 0 00 219403 1
Filmset by Jolly & Barber Ltd, Rugby, Warwickshire
Printed in Great Britain by Butler & Tanner Ltd, Frome, Somerset

Contents

Preface

The great oceans and the seas which cover more than half of the surface of the world form the home of the majority of seabirds, except for those periods when they take to the land to breed. The areas in which they breed range from the very outposts of the high arctic and antarctic regions to isolated tropical islands and the cliffs and headlands bordering widely dispersed continental coasts.

The sea creates no barrier for seabirds, save that in different zones the upper layers of the sea provide food suited to particular species.

Many species of seabird disperse from their congested breeding locations when their nesting is completed and fly to more favourable latitudes. In particular those truly oceanic species which breed in high northern and southern latitudes may undertake long trans-equatorial migrations during their contra-nuptial seasons.

The voyage narratives in this volume stem from a study of many thousands of positive observations of bird movements made at differing seasons over a period of more than twenty years, observations made by the untiring members of the Royal Naval and Mercantile Marine Birdwatching Society and other persons taking part in the society's worldwide reporting system. To all who may glance through this book and may recognise some quotation or detail extracted from their sea passage reports or letters I tender my grateful thanks.

G.S.T.

Introduction

When land has disappeared and the open sea stretches on all sides the ocean voyager may wonder at the apparent emptiness of the sea and sky. On the ocean routes days often pass without another vessel being sighted. Perhaps, now and again, a school of dolphins will be seen as they plunge through the crests of the waves or cut across the stern of the ship, the glitter of flying fish may be glimpsed as they skim above the waves in the sunshine or the cry go up of 'There she blows!' as the dark grey back of a whale breaks the surface of the ocean. However, to the aware observer there is much more to be seen for the seabirds are a ship's true companions and a constantly changing pattern of seabird life unfolds as a vessel makes its voyage.

A traveller aboard a ship following one of the normal sea routes is unlikely to be fortunate enough to see all the seabirds which frequent the geographical areas which border the route on either side. Some species, the gulls for example, do not range far from the coast and the ship may pass well outside their habitual foraging area, and migratory species may only be present at a particular season. There will be times when a remarkable concentration of seabirds will appear and new and exciting species be seen for the first time but, on other occasions, it will be easy for a bird to pass unnoticed unless a keen watch is kept and on some sea routes days may pass without a single seabird being sighted.

This book describes, in narrative form, the species which are most likely to appear along a particular sea route in the order in which they may be seen from leaving a given port of departure to the ultimate port of arrival. Twenty-five of the principal ocean routes are so described. The book forms a complementary volume to the author's *A Field Guide to the Seabirds of Britain and the World*, which is planned as a handy means of identifying each species. In the description of each ocean route a species, when mentioned for the first time, is given in its usual English form followed, in brackets, by the plate number of the coloured illustration which depicts it in the *Field Guide*. In addition information to assist in species identification is included in this narrative, although not in such detail as in the *Field Guide*.

Not every reader of this book will be an expert ornithologist and the following brief outline is offered to explain the basis of classification, the general characteristics of seabird families, oceanic distribution, plumage variation and other topics of which a general understanding will aid the reader.

CLASSIFICATION

Seabirds, in common with all other animals and plants, are classified systematically under separate ORDERS, each based primarily upon a similarity of anatomical structure. The individual Orders are subdivided into separate FAMILIES and within each Family an individual seabird is identified according to its GENUS (race) and SPECIES. Thus, for example, the Lesser Black-backed Gull is of the Order Charadriiformes, within the Family Laridae, and its scientific name, *Larus fuscus*, indicates that it belongs to the Genus *Larus* and the Species *fuscus* (the genetic and specific names together giving the scientific name of the species). Many books,

7

especially scholarly works and text books, show the scientific name after the species' vernacular name so that it may be accurately identified no matter what language the book is written in or what form of the common name is used.

Sub-specific Titles

Birds of the same species which occur in different geographical areas in certain cases have developed small differences in physical characteristics and plumage and accordingly have been allotted sub-specific titles giving them a three-part name. To the birdwatcher at sea, observing species on the wing, these minor differences are insufficient to make exact identification to sub-species possible. Indeed, in some cases there is disagreement between the experts on the exact allocation of sub-specific names.

PRIMARY AND SECONDARY SEABIRDS

Seabirds have been divided into primary and secondary categories, the division being broadly according to their normal habitat. The former are those whose normal habitat may be regarded as the sea. The latter are those which usually live on lagoons, inland lakes and estuaries and include such birds as grebes, divers and most sea ducks. These secondary seabirds are very rarely seen on the ocean routes and, with the exception of the phalaropes, which spend most of the winter months at sea, will not be found included in the route lists.

SEABIRD FAMILIES – GENERAL CHARACTERISTICS

The different species of seabirds which are classified within the same Family will be seen to possess the general characteristics of the Family within which they are placed and these characteristics will provide the first clue to their identity before trying to determine their species. Naturally, the first object on sighting a seabird will be to identify it and the following general characteristics will aid recognition of the different Families.

PENGUINS. Family: Spheniscidae. Medium to outsize birds, Penguins have stout bodies and short necks. On land they stand upright on short, webbed feet which are set far back on their bodies. They differ from all other seabirds in having 'flippers' instead of quilled wings. When at the surface Penguins swim very low in the water with only the head or part of the back showing and they are sometimes seen 'porpoising' in and out of the water. They are confined to the Southern Hemisphere, with the exception of one species which breeds on the Galapagos Islands.

ALBATROSSES AND MOLLYMAWKS. Family: Driomedeidae.   These very large to outsize birds are recognised at sea by their size, long slender wings, stout bills (which have the upper mandible slightly hooked), short tails and characteristic gliding flight. Species identification is aided by the different colour patterns of their bills. The smaller species are often referred to as 'Mollymawks'.

TRUE PETRELS AND SHEARWATERS. Family: Procellariidae.   These birds are of medium size and have long, narrow wings which are held out straight or angled in flight. They usually fly low over the sea, in some cases banking and upswinging on extended wings. At close quarters True Petrels and Shearwaters can be distinguished by their tubular nostrils. The six Prions, smaller than most other Petrels, are light blue-grey above with a dark W-shaped pattern across the upper wings. Their underparts are white and their wedge-shaped tails terminate in a black band. Confined principally to the southern oceans, the six species are indistinguishable under normal viewing conditions at sea and are best referred to as *Prions* sp. At sea they are usually seen in flocks, flying swiftly and twisting from side to side.

STORM PETRELS. Family: Hydrobatidae. These very small, usually dark, seabirds may frequently be seen flitting back and forth near to the sea's surface, sometimes following closely in the wake of a ship, or pattering the surface with their webbed feet when feeding. Storm Petrels can be distinguished at very close quarters by their tubular nostrils or the shape of their tails.

DIVING PETRELS. Family: Pelecanoididae. These small, stumpy little birds are blackish above and white below with short bills. Their wings and legs are placed well back on their bodies. They are usually seen in flocks, resting on the surface or flying short distances with rapidly-beating wings, and diving or alighting. They are confined to southern oceans and have tubular nostrils and a distensible pouch between the sides of the lower mandible which they fill with food to carry to their chicks.

TROPIC-BIRDS. Family: Phaethontidae. Tropic-birds are white birds of medium size and are extremely graceful with greatly elongated central tail feathers. They are high flying and beat their wings with great speed and power. Immature Tropic Birds have much-reduced tail streamers.

PELICANS. Family: Pelecanidae. These birds are very large and have broad, rounded wings, heavy bodies and huge, pouched bills. In flight their heads and necks are thrust back on to the shoulders. They plunge clumsily into the sea for food or, in some cases, can be seen swimming in tight formation close inshore to drive fish into shallow water.

GANNETS AND BOOBIES. Family: Sulidae. These are very large, cigar-shaped birds with long, narrow wings, short necks and stout, conically-pointed bills. In flight they look extremely stately and their wing beats are very regular. They plunge headlong into the sea for food. It is the pan-tropical species which are known as Boobies.

CORMORANTS AND SHAGS. Family: Phalacrocoracidae. Medium to large in size, these are dark birds with long necks and wings and long slender bills which are strongly hooked. Their legs are placed far back and their tails are stiff. They usually fly low over the sea with regular wing beats and dive from the surface to swim underwater to catch fish. They may often be seen on posts or seamarks with their wings extended to dry.

FRIGATE BIRDS. Family: Fregatidae. Frigate Birds are very large and have almost black plumage. Their wings are very long and they have long, forked tails and long hooked bills. They will circle overhead for hours, tails opening and closing in a scissor-like way to assist their balance. They will chase other seabirds, harrying them until they disgorge their catch, which the Frigate Bird will snatch before it reaches the water.

PHALAROPES. Family: Phalaropodidae. These wading birds are very small and delicate. They breed in the far northern tundra and spend the non-breeding winter months entirely at sea in a number of warmer-sea areas where their plankton food is rich. They have long, slender necks and carry them very upright when they are swimming. They are usually seen at sea in winter plumage, in flocks riding buoyantly on the surface or, when disturbed, flying for short distances with rapid wing beats.

SKUAS AND JAEGERS. Family: Stercorariidae.   These medium-sized birds are a uniform dark brown or, in their pale phase, have yellowish sides to head and neck and pale underparts. They have long wings and stout, slightly hooked bills. The Great Skua is much larger than the three smaller skuas, or Jaegers as they are often called. It is brown with pale patches on the outer areas of the broad, rounded wings. The smaller Jaegers have long, pointed wings, wedge-shaped tails and short, protruding central tail feathers. Their flight is like that of the falcon. All species chase and pirate other seabirds. The Long-tailed Skua has no dark phase and its central tail feathers are particularly elongated.

GULLS. Family: Laridae.   These birds are medium to large in size and can be distinguished by their long, narrow wings, short legs and square tails. In the breeding season most species have plumage of mixed grey and white with, in some cases, a black head.

TERNS. Family: Sternidae.   A few species, the Noddies for example, are mainly sooty-brown. Sooty and Bridled Terns have dark upper wings and white foreheads. Terns fly with rapid wingbeats. When searching for food they hover and then plunge into the sea.

SKIMMERS. Family: Rhynchopidae.   These medium-sized birds have very long, narrow wings, short legs, and slightly-forked tails. Their overall appearance is very like that of the terns, although larger. Their plumage is blackish above with white underparts and white foreheads. Their long bills are usually orange or yellow, with darker tips, and the lower mandible extends much further forward than the upper one.

AUKS. Family: Alcidae.   Auks are small to medium-sized birds with short wings. Their plumage is usually dark above and white below. In flight their wings are flapped rapidly and they never appear to travel far in the air. They float high on the water and obtain food by diving from the surface, using their wings to propel them below the surface.

GENERAL

The details given above will help the reader to identify the family to which a bird belongs when it is initially sighted, but, to make a positive identification of an individual species it will be necessary to concentrate upon the details of the colour and pattern of the plumage. The colours of the upperparts, underparts, underwings and other characteristics are not easy to see when a bird is on the wing. A good pair of binoculars of, say, 7×50 magnification and diameter will be found essential for making an accurate indentification. Binoculars of higher magnification and smaller field have the disadvantage that under the roll and movement of a ship at sea it is difficult to hold the target in vision.

The serious observer should look out for the following points and enter such details in a notebook. More leisurely identification can then be made later and a permanent record is available for future reference. If you have drawing skill an accompanying sketch will prove useful and may make it easier to note features by means of arrows to the drawing rather than having to write down descriptions. If positive identification of species is easily made it will not, of course, be necessary to record all these features.

1. Size and build   Size: very large, large, medium or small. Build: heavy, compact, light or slender.

2. Type of flight.   Wings: straight or angled. Wing beats: slow, rapid, fluttering or gliding on fixed pinions.
3. Wings.   Short and broad or long and narrow.
4. Tail.   Very long, short and round, square or wedge-shaped.
5. Plumage colour.   *a*) head, *b*) back and upperwing, *c*) underparts and under-wing, *d*) rump, *e*) tail, *f*) colour and shape of bill and legs.
6. Behaviour and voice.   Behaviour: solitary, in flocks, active or sluggish. Voice: noisy or silent.

ESTIMATING SIZE. Length is measured from the tip of the bill to the tip of the longest tail feather. In Tropic Birds the length of the central tail streamers may also be added separately, for in immature and young birds the length is very much reduced.

Description	Length ins.	mm.	Description	Length ins.	mm.
Tiny	4–6	102–152	Medium–Large	20–24	508–609
Very Small	6–8	152–203	Large	24–28	609–711
Small	8–12	203–305	Very Large	28–32	711–813
Small–Medium	12–16	305–406	Outsize	Above 32	Above 813
Medium	16–20	406–508			

WING SPAN is measured between the outer tips of both wings when they are fully outstretched.

DISTRIBUTION

Some seabirds tend to stay closer to land than others and identification of species will be made easier by a knowledge of which species can be classed 'INSHORE,' 'OFFSHORE,' or 'OCEANIC,' even though these terms can be considered only as guides.

INSHORE. Gulls, Pelicans, Terns and Noddies closer to land. Sooty and Brown-winged or Bridle Terns, however, are often seen far out to sea.

OFFSHORE. Gannets, Boobies, Frigate Birds, Cormorants and Auks generally feed further offshore but, together with Tropic Birds, individual Boobies often range well out to sea.

OCEANIC. Once you are out in the open ocean you will observe that the inshore and offshore species give way to the truly oceanic seabirds: the Albatrosses, Petrels, Fulmer Petrels, Shearwaters, Storm Petrels, Kittiwakes and Prions.

All birds nest and rear their young on land and during the breeding seasons, when adult breeding birds collect at their breeding colonies, both oceanic and offshore species will appear close inshore, immature non-breeders mostly remaining at sea.

GEOGRAPHICAL DISTRIBUTIONS

The geographical distribution of seabirds around the globe depends on many different factors. Only a few of the principal ones can be mentioned here.

Seabirds of particular species tend to spread laterally around the globe within their own most favourable climatic belts: arctic, antarctic, temperate or tropical latitudes. In some instances, however, certain species which breed within high latitudes of one hemisphere will undertake enormously long trans-equatorial migrations, after their breeding season, to spend non-breeding periods within similar latitudes in the opposing hemisphere. In general, however, we find the majority of Gulls favouring the northern and southern temperate latitude belts, more particularly in the northern belt because of its extensive land masses. Others, such as the Boobies, Frigate Birds, Pelicans, Tropic Birds and tropical terns are to be found spread across the tropical zones of the oceans, whilst other species belong to the arctic and antarctic latitudes.

Within these broad latitude belts different species of ocean birds will range and congregate in areas of high surface feed.

The density of oceanic seabird life is dependent upon the availability of surface planktonic food on which many fish and crustacea feed before themselves becoming the food of carnivores. The greatest concentrations of the nutrient salts upon which the plankton itself thrives are brought up to the surface, from the depths in which they settle, where deep cold currents move upwards, displacing warmer waters, in a pattern known as 'upwelling'. Food is therefore likely to be richer in areas of greatest turbulence. Such conditions occur in Antarctic and Arctic seas, created where cold currents sweep northwards from the Antarctic along the coasts of South America in the Humboldt Current and Falkland Current, in the Benguela Current up the west coast of South Africa, and also up the western coast of Australia. They also occur in areas where opposing currents meet, for example, where the southward flowing Labrador Current meets the Gulf Stream, where Equatorial and Counter Equatorial Currents mingle, and also where currents off land masses cause upwelling, as does the southward flowing Canaries Current. Air currents also have their effect. A noteworthy example is that of the South West Monsoon which causes upwelling offshore from the coasts of south-east Arabia.

The greatest variety and concentration of oceanic seabirds are likely to be observed in such areas and under such conditions, particularly during periods of seasonal migration.

PLUMAGE DIFFERENCES IN SEABIRDS

With the exception of a few species, seabirds on the wing do not show any noticeable sexual differentiation. Among the exceptions are the Frigate Birds, the females of which, save for the Ascension Frigate Bird, show differing areas of white on their underparts. However, young and immature birds often have entirely different plumage from that of full adults of the same species. Many immatures take several years to assume their full adult plumage. One of the most obvious cases concerns some of the Albatrosses in which immatures take several years to develop from their initial, almost overall brownish, plumage to the final adult phase. This is also particularly noticeable in the case of the Gulls.

The majority of adult oceanic seabirds retain the same plumage throughout the year, moult feathers being replaced by feathers of similar colour, but there are a number of exceptions, among them the Phalaropes and the Auks which have distinct summer and winter plumage. Black and brown-headed gulls and terns lose their breeding hoods or crowns in autumn and winter, leaving only a dusky streak about their heads. There is also a tendency in birds with brightly-coloured bills and legs to revert to duller colours in winter plumage.

For fuller details reference should be made to the *Field Guide*.

PREPARING FOR A VOYAGE

A traveller will do well to study the complete narrative of a particular voyage before embarking, consulting an atlas to see the actual route in its various stages and noting the sequence in which those species most likely to be observed may possibly appear.

RECORDING OBSERVATIONS

In keeping a record of birds observed during a voyage it is best to follow a form of recording each separate sighting using consecutive numbers for each observation as the voyage proceeds. A note should be made recording positive or uncertain identification for each species and adult or immature bird as appropriate. In practice it will usually be sufficient for the position of the ship at daylight, noon and dusk (local times) to be noted (information which can be obtained from the ship's Navigating Officer) and the nearest of these positions in latitude and longitude recorded for the respective observations. When land or islands are in sight it is helpful to indicate the bearing and distance of any such named landmarks at the approximate time of observations.

SEABIRDS ON BOARD

Unless injured or incapacitated, seabirds have no need to land on board, no matter what the sea and weather conditions may be. However, certain species do make use of a ship, particularly the Boobies. These birds frequently alight on ships at some vantage point from which they can keep a sharp look-out for flying fish, ready to launch themselves, capture and devour any that break surface from the ship's bows. They have been known to remain on board at sea for this purpose for days on end.

Tropic Birds are a species which follow in the wake of ships at night, waiting to capture squid that have been disturbed in the ship's wake. On such occasions they frequently become dazzled by the ship's lights, colliding with parts of its structure, and may be found dazed or damaged on deck. Once on deck, even if uninjured, they are unable to take-off by themselves. Storm Petrels also appear to follow ships in the dark at times in search of pickings and may be found on board in similar sorry circumstances.

Seabirds found bedraggled or injured on board

Seabirds found injured or bedraggled should immediately be placed on a piece of cloth in a cardboard box with plenty of ventilation holes and then put in a warm place to allow them to recover their composure (or to dry off). Later they should be inspected in the hope that they may have recovered sufficiently to launch them into flight over the ship's side. It is unwise to place them in water but the opportunity can be taken, at discretion, to tempt the larger species with small pieces of chopped-up raw fish, or, in the case of Storm Petrels, to feed them with cod liver oil, using a pipette to dispense it slowly. Drinking water can also be made available.

Treatment of oiled seabirds on board ships at sea

An increasing number of seabirds contaminated with oil are arriving on board ships at sea. Ships do not offer suitable conditions for lengthy rehabilitation to be undertaken but the following action end treatment has proved successful in several cases.

Attempts to clean the bird should not immediately be started. At first the bird should be kept warm and quiet. It should be securely wrapped in a cloth, with only its head and legs protruding, to prevent it preening and thus swallowing more oil, and then placed in a suitable cardboard box with ventilation. The feet should be treated with a little ointment or hand cream to prevent cracking.

TREATMENT. After the bird has rested an attempt should be made, before beginning to treat the oil, to feed or force-feed suitable food. After that carefully wash the affected parts in a warm solution of commercial 'washing-up' liquid: 1.5cc of detergent to 1 litre (⅛ pint to 1 gallon) of hand-hot water at about 40.5*C (105*F), holding the affected parts submerged and separating the feathers. It will usually be necessary to perform a second washing with a fresh solution. Finally rinse out all the detergent in hand-hot water. Dry by mopping with a clean cloth or hold the bird in front of a warm air duct, then return the bird to its covered box and place it somewhere really warm, for example under a hot towel rail, where it may rest.

As the bird gains strength and mobility continue feeding and allow it to preen. It will not be recovered sufficiently to be launched into the air until it has begun to flap its wings and show clearly that it is ready and eager to fly away.

Outward Bound from Scandinavian, Baltic and Eastern North Sea Ports

Unlike the progressive appearance of different species of seabirds which is a feature of most long ocean routes, the species occurring in the local sea areas around these Baltic and eastern North Sea ports, with a few exceptions, are liable to be seen in all of them although in varying quantity. The narrative therefore aims at providing a more general outline rather than selecting a particular shipping route.

Those species likely to be seen most frequently in harbours or close inshore are discussed first rather than adhering to their strict systematic order.

GULLS. Certain species breed throughout the area from the far north coast of Norway to the British Isles and we may consider these first. Here we find the **Great Black-backed Gull (27, 34, 40)**, the **Herring Gull (28, 35, 40)**, the **Lesser Black-backed Gull (27, 34, 35, 40)** and the **Common Gull (28, 35, 40)**. Two races of Herring Gull overlap; on the northern coasts of Norway, principally somewhat north of 60°N., and in the Baltic one may expect to see a yellow-legged race, *Larus argentatus omissus*, while in the southern areas the race with flesh-coloured legs. Similarly a northern race of the Lesser Black-backed Gull, *Larus fuscus fuscus* (34) occurs, having a darker almost black mantle and bright yellow legs compared with the dark slate grey mantle and duller yellow legs of the more southerly race, *Larus f. graellsii* (35). On the eastern seaboard the Great and Lesser Black-backed Gulls breed in the British Isles and principally northwards from the Kattegat. The Lesser Black-backed Gull breeds however in Holland, Denmark, commonly on the coasts of Norway and northwards on the Baltic coasts. The Herring Gull breeds freely

Kittiwake

15

along all the coastlines, with very large numbers in Holland, on the North Sea coasts of Germany, the Baltic and northwards to the extreme north of Norway. The Common Gull breeds in the British Isles, and in smaller numbers in Holland for its summer range is further north. Very large numbers breed in Germany, Denmark, through Norway, Sweden and the Baltic.

The **Northern Black-headed Gull (28, 31, 32, 37, 40)** has a somewhat more southerly range, breeding freely in the British Isles and Holland, thence northwards to the southern coasts of Norway, Sweden and eastern coasts of the Baltic.

Of all the gulls, the **Common Kittiwake (33, 39)** is the most oceanic, keeping solely to the sea and open ocean outside the breeding season. Unlike many other gulls, it is unlikely to be seen inland. A large number breed in the British Isles, a few in Denmark. They seek precipitous cliffs on which to breed, and colonise the Atlantic coast of Norway, colonies extending to islands in the high arctic. Common Kittiwakes tend to disperse westwards into the N. Atlantic and, while plentiful off the coasts of the British Isles and Norway, are somewhat less commonly seen elsewhere in the eastern quarter of the North Sea. Adults can be distinguished from other gulls at sea by their more slender appearance, more buoyant flight and the completely black tips to their pearl-grey upperwings. Immatures show a black band on the hindneck, a distinctive black diagonal band on the upperwing and a black terminal band on the tail. One other gull which breeds in the high arctic, the **Glaucous Gull (29, 35, 40)**, disperses southwards through the Norwegian Sea in winter months and may be seen off the Norwegian coast. Its large size and very pale, almost cream-coloured mantle, white primaries, yellow bill and flesh-coloured legs distinguish it from other gulls at sea in the area.

Ships leaving Norwegian ports will not see the **Little Gull (31, 32, 37)** for this small gull is only an occasional breeder in Holland, extending as a breeding species chiefly from Denmark through the Baltic States. It is but a passing visitor through the east coast of Britain and the Low Countries, and winters in the Mediterranean. In adult breeding plumage its neat compact appearance, somewhat rounded jet-black head and throat, pure white rather rounded upperwings and distinctive dark slate-grey underwings should be looked for. Immatures have a very variable mottled plumage, a black bar across wings and white underwings in their first and second years.

TERNS. Terns are seen infrequently in the open sea, mainly on migration, and are exceedingly difficult to identify by species as they pass overhead. It is between early spring and late summer before their southward departure that they may be seen in their breeding colonies or close off the shore line plunging into shallow waters to capture small fry.

With the exception of the **Arctic Tern (41, 42)**, whose breeding range extends into arctic Norway and the high arctic, and the **Common Tern (42, 43)** into northern Norway, the remaining terns within the area breed further south where the east coast of Britain and eastern shores of the North and Baltic Seas provide stretches of sand dunes and marshes. The Arctic Tern breeds in the northern parts of the British Isles, barely touches the Netherlands, extending from the north German coast to Denmark, Norway, Sweden and the Baltic. The Common Tern breeds in the British Isles, in very large colonies in Holland and Germany, thence northwards throughout the area. The **Sandwich Tern (41, 43)** has a more southerly breeding range, the greatest proportion breeding in Holland. In the British Isles and Germany it is a regular breeder with small numbers in Denmark and Sweden. The

Little Tern (43) breeds in diminishing numbers in the British Isles, is absent from Norway, and occurs through Holland, Germany and the Baltic. The **Roseate Tern (42)** is almost entirely confined as a breeder to the British Isles within the area.

This completes the more common species of terns; there are others whose occurrence is less well defined. The **Black Tern (44)** breeds through Holland, Germany, Denmark and the Baltic. The **Whiskered Tern (44)**, possibly now absent, and the **Gull-billed Tern (43)** have occurred in Holland. Like the Black Tern, both are marsh-loving species rarely seen at sea.

THE AUK FAMILY (Alcidae). This family of seabirds is seen to best advantage in large colonies at their cliff nesting sites on stacks, ledges, or in the case of **Atlantic Puffins (47)** outside their burrows. The small **Black Guillemot (46)** is more solitary, only a few pairs usually nesting in any one locality either in crevices or under the shelter of boulders at the foot of rocky coastlines.

With the exception of the **Little Auk (46)**, they are primarily offshore seabirds, but the Atlantic Puffin, **Common Guillemot** and **Razorbill (46)** may all be seen on coastal passages in the area out of sight of land.

In the eastern Atlantic the Little Auk breeds on Iceland and arctic islands north of Norway but disperses southwards during autumn and winter months through the Norwegian Sea. Under normal circumstances it is oceanic. Occasions have occurred not infrequently after severe north-westerly gales for flights to be seen well within sight of land, not only off the coast of Norway, but extending to the northern area of the British Isles and into the North Sea. These stubby little short-winged auks sometimes become wrecked inland in exceptional storms.

Common Guillemots breed in large colonies on the coast of Norway, in Denmark, in large numbers in Sweden, lesser numbers in Germany, and in the British Isles. The northern form of the Common Guillemot *Uria aalge aalge*, which breeds on the coast of Norway, has almost black upperparts contrasting with the dark chocolate-brown upperparts of the southern race. Razorbills occur in similar areas in smaller numbers. Apart from Iceland and the Faroes the largest breeding populations of the Atlantic Puffin are on the north and west coasts of the British Isles and adjacent islands and also on the Atlantic coast of Norway. The Atlantic Puffin does not occur in the Baltic. The Black Guillemot occurs sparsely in the extreme north of the British Isles, in the Kattegat and coasts of Norway, Sweden and the Baltic.

GANNETS. The **Northern Gannet (18)**, the largest seabird in the N. Atlantic, is confined to very large breeding colonies surrounding the British Isles, Shetland and the Faroes, with outlying colonies in Iceland. While birds from the more southern breeding areas tend to disperse southwards towards the bulge of N. Africa, a number of the northern breeding birds certainly disperse northwards. Northern Gannets are regular deep sea wanderers and ships operating from ports may expect to sight them in ones or twos, more particularly from the northern quarter of the North Sea as far north as the Arctic Circle.

CORMORANTS and SHAGS. Two races of the **Common Cormorant (20, 23)** occur. The race *Phalacrocorax carbo carbo* breeds northwards to Iceland and the Atlantic coast of Norway. Another race, *Phalacrocorax c. sinensis* **(20)**, takes its place in Denmark, Holland and Belgium, thence southwards. Both species are almost identical except in the breeding season only when *Phalacrocorax c. sinensis* shows a white head extending down the neck. In the breeding season the white patches on the thighs are noticeable. Common Cormorants and **Shags (21)** do not wander far

Northern Gannet

from the coast and the commoner Cormorant often penetrates harbours, rivers and lakes. The Shag breeds in the British Isles and along the full length of the Atlantic Norwegian coast, but is unlikely to be seen in other areas at sea, remaining closer to the cliffs.

SKUAS. All four species, the **Great, Arctic, Pomarine** and **Long-tailed Skuas (26)**, may be seen occasionally at sea in the area during their northerly and southerly migrations, usually during May and June and from late August to mid-October. The Great Skua, as large as a Herring Gull, with a rusty-brown plumage, shows conspicuous pale wing patches in flight. It breeds further south than the other species on islands north of the British Isles, extending to Iceland and parts of Norway. The Arctic Skua breeds from the Shetland Is. northwards to high arctic islands and northern coasts of Europe and arctic Russia. Both the Pomarine and Long-tailed Skuas breed in the highest arctic latitudes. Pomarine and Arctic Skuas have two plumage phases, a light phase with a dark cap, yellowish neck and pale underbody showing a dark breast band, and a dark phase in which the whole plumage is uniformly brown. They are best distinguished when not in moult by the shape of their short protruding central tail feathers. The Long-tailed Skua can be said to have no dark phase and its elongated central tail feathers are most noticeable. These three smaller skuas are more lightly built and more hawk-like in appearance and flight than the Great Skua.

PETRELS, SHEARWATERS AND STORM-PETRELS. The outstanding petrel of the area is the **Northern Fulmar (11)** whose original breeding station was the island of St Kilda but which now breeds extensively in the British Isles and has extended its range down the east coast. Breeding colonies also occur on the Atlantic coast of Norway and beyond into the high arctic. This highly oceanic species, like the Common Kittiwake, ranges widely at sea outside the breeding season, and indeed large numbers are to be seen at sea at all times of the year. They are seen regularly in the North Sea, less numbers in the eastern quarter, and are the principal feature

Fulmar

together with the Common Kittiwake seen by ships trading off the coast of Norway as far as the North Cape and beyond. They do not however normally penetrate to the approaches of the Baltic. Birds occurring in the southern zone are of the pale phase type while off the northern coasts of Norway some may be seen in the dark phase, commonly known as 'Blue' Fulmars. In the higher arctic regions a greater proportion are dark birds. Seen among gulls and Common Kittiwakes congregating around fishing vessels, they are easily recognised by their magnificent flight, planing on stiffly held wings making use of every variation of wind current.

The **Manx Shearwater (9)** and the **British** and **Leach's Storm-petrels (13)** all breed on the western coasts and islands off the British Isles, but their range at sea extends to the west and north-west and they are unlikely to be seen by ships at any distance to the east of the British Isles.

The extreme northerly range of the **Sooty Shearwater (8)** and **Wilson's Storm-petrel (13)** on conclusion of their enormous migrations from the southern oceans very rarely extends so far east although on rare occasions in the late summer the Sooty Shearwater has been seen by ships in the deep water areas off Norway.

PHALAROPES. These dainty little waders are discussed last in this survey for their occurrence at sea is infrequent and irregular on migration. Apart from their brief breeding season near open pools in the highest northern latitudes, they spend some seven months of the year at sea in certain favoured areas in the equatorial belt of the oceans. The thick underdown on their bodies and fringed webs to their toes make them well adapted for life at sea. The **Grey Phalarope (25)** breeds in the highest possible northern latitudes around the polar basin and yet has one breeding area in S. Iceland. A few occur occasionally at sea in the area on migration but records from ships are exceedingly scarce. The breeding range of the **Red-necked Phalarope (25)** is less northerly for it breeds extensively in central and northern Norway and Iceland. Limited numbers extend further southward to breed in the Faroes,

Shetland and Orkney Is. and in the Outer Hebrides. Like the Grey Phalarope, it is rarely seen at sea on migration.

At sea on passage

Ships come and go on different routes from ports in the area and will see many similar species. From a summary of observations one route may serve as an example, a ship on passage from the Kattegat northwards to the North Cape.

Lesser Black-backed Gulls, Herring Gulls and Northern Black-headed Gulls will follow at the outset, the Common Gull less frequently. Close alone the shore line Cormorants may be seen, and in the breeding season Common Guillemots and Razorbills flying with whirring flight to and from their breeding colonies. Once well clear of the land the smaller gulls are likely to be left behind but the Herring Gull, Great and Lesser Black-backed Gulls will continue to follow. As the ship proceeds northwards Common Kittiwakes and Northern Fulmars will appear and together with Herring Gulls will be seen throughout the passage. Where fishing vessels are operating, Great and Lesser Black-backed Gulls may join the throng and an occasional Northern Gannet at any time of the year. If the passage occurs in May and June or late August and September, a lookout should also be kept for passing skuas, the Pomarine, Arctic and Long-tailed Skuas having been noted as far as the North Cape.

Off the northern coasts of Norway, Common Guillemots, Razorbills and Atlantic Puffins are plentiful, spreading further from the coasts outside the breeding season. Terns are occasionally seen on spring and autumn passage, and although difficult to identify are most likely to be Arctic Terns. Here too a lookout should be kept for the Glaucous Gull and Little Auk. There is of course some overlap between summer and winter seasons. Common Kittiwakes, for example, largely forsake the open ocean between June and late August while at their breeding colonies but the number of Northern Fulmars far out at sea at this season appears to remain unchanged.

On this route however from March through May and again from late August through October, practically every seabird quoted might be encountered.

Leaving Harbour
from The British Isles

Wharves, docks and harbours where ships lie and garbage collects provide an irresistible attraction to the inshore feeding gulls. Some or all of the following are almost sure to be seen wheeling around the ship's berth, the more resolute **Herring Gull (28, 35, 40)** and **Lesser Black-backed Gull (27, 35, 40)** settling on the ship's gunwhales while the more wary **Northern Black-headed Gull (28, 31, 32, 37, 40)** and **Common Gull (28, 35, 40)** keep their distance back and forth along the vessel's side.

Lesser Black-backed and Herring Gulls

The outstandingly large **Great Black-backed Gull (27, 34, 40)** is more solitary than the smaller gulls, preferring open rocky coastlines to ports and docks, and is more likely to be seen in the autumn and winter months.

A number of these resident inshore gulls are to some extent partial migrants within the British Isles moving southwards during the autumn and winter months and resorting to inland reservoirs, sewage farms and town refuse dumps. The Common Gull, which breeds in the northern areas, will be seen rarely in southern ports in spring and summer, while a considerable proportion of the Lesser Black-backed Gulls leave the British Isles in the winter for warmer climates further south.

A first clue to their identity in adult plumage will be the greater size, leisurely wing-beat and sooty-black mantle and upperwings of the Great Black-backed Gull, the dark slate-grey upperwings of the Lesser Black-backed Gull, the grey of the Herring Gull, and the pale grey of the smaller Common Gull. The plumage of the Northern Black-headed Gull is however distinctive.

Birds in immature plumage may frequently appear to outnumber full adults for it will be some years before the immature mottled brownish plumage of the three larger gulls has been finally discarded, and identification in their first and second years' immature plumage needs careful discrimination.

Terns breeding in the British Isles

The British Isles can claim no terns which are resident throughout the year. All the terns described and to be seen around the British Isles during the spring and summer months have arrived from more southern latitudes to occupy established breeding colonies on sand dunes, marshes, reed-fringed lakes or islets. On completion of the breeding season adults and immatures alike depart. Rare species unlikely to be seen are omitted.

It is unusual to see terns in our ports for there is nothing in the scraps of food around the docks to attract them. Their food consists chiefly of small live fish and sand eels for which they may be seen plunging into shallow water close offshore.

On the whole, terns are seen rarely by ships leaving direct to the open sea, and it is in coastal waters near their breeding colonies that the best opportunity of identifying them may present itself. Only a few terns of those quoted range far out to sea except during migration. On such occasions they keep clear of ships, and so similar are they in appearance seen at some distance at sea that identification of individual species is on many occasions impossible.

Sandwich Tern (41, 43). The largest of the British breeding terns with more elongated black feathers on the crown. Its harsh call note 'kirrick' may give a clue to its identity.

Sandwich Tern

Common Tern (42, 43) and **Arctic Tern (41, 42).** The two species are so similar in general appearance that observation at close quarters is necessary to distinguish between them. Their call notes are also very similar, a high-pitched 'keee yaah' or 'kik-kik-kik', quite distinctive from that of the Sandwich Tern.

Roseate Tern (42). Tends to cling to the land but when seen in company with Common or Arctic Terns looks much whiter and has a distinctive grating 'aach-aach' call note.

Little Tern (43). Noticeably smaller than the Common and Arctic Terns, and more easily identified by its rapid wing-beats and call note 'kirri-kikki, kirri-kikki' or 'kyik'.

Little Tern

British Isles to
East Coasts of Canada and U.S.A.

The sea area considered covers that bounded in the north by the track from the north of Ireland in latitude 56°N. to the Belle Isle Strait in latitude 52°N., and in the south by the track from the English Channel in latitude 50°N. to New York in latitude 41°N.

From approximately June to November, when the Belle Isle Strait is ice-free, ships on passage to the Gulf of St Lawrence usually make use of the northerly route through this Strait. From December to May, when ice blocks the Strait, the route via Cape Race and the Cabot Strait is in use. Ships bound for New York follow a more southerly route south of the Newfoundland Grand Banks thence direct to their destination.

Many N. Atlantic seabirds, including those which pass northwards and southwards during seasonal migrations, are common to all three routes. Each route however shows certain differences in the variety and quantity of the species which occur.

Seabirds common to all three routes at all seasons at the outset of the voyages

For ships on the New York run, the passage down the English Channel is described in Route 9 (p. 51).

Before a ship leaving a northern port through the North Channel has cleared the land, and while most of the gulls which have followed out of harbour are still

Northern Gannet

escorting the ship, several more seabirds are likely to be seen. From ships passing down the Firth of Clyde a lookout must surely be kept on passing Ailsa Craig, one of the great breeding colonies of the **Northern Gannet (18)**. During the breeding season the sloping sides of the island are white with gannets. The white adults with their black wing tips will be seen coming and going with steady majestic flight, or in the distance plummeting into the sea as they dive for fish.

Close offshore the **Common Cormorant (20, 23)** and possibly the **Shag (21)** may be seen. Neither feed at any distance to seaward; sometimes when fishing they appear suddenly with their necks alone showing, or at other times are seen flying low over the sea with black necks extended. In harbour they are partial to perching on posts and beacons, their dark wings outstretched.

The **Atlantic Puffin (47)**, **Razorbill (46)** and **Common Guillemot (46)** may all be seen in the North Channel and while rounding the coast of N. Ireland until Inishtrahull I. is left astern. With the exception of the **Black Guillemot (46)**, they are

Puffin

all dark above with white underparts, fly with direct whirring flight and dive frequently. At sea at a distance Razorbills and guillemots in particular can be confused easily. The smaller Black Guillemot is rarely seen as it clings close to the coast, but it might be seen off the coast of N. Ireland, in the Gulf of St Lawrence or on the northern coasts of U.S.A.

The open ocean

Once in the open ocean, and perhaps after the last Northern Gannet has been seen, the offshore seabirds will be replaced by oceanic species. Undoubtedly the two species most abundant over the two northern routes will be the **Common Kittiwake (33, 39)** and **Northern Fulmar (11)**. The Northern Fulmar is a good deal less frequent over the more southern route to New York. Rarely a day passes on the Canadian routes without both species being seen close to the ship.

The seasonal pattern of their distribution calls for some amplification resulting from day to day monthly counts undertaken by the British Ocean Weather Ships

Razorbill

over several years. Through the year, Northern Fulmars always outnumber Common Kittiwakes out in the ocean, the latter generally being only half as numerous, although both species are plentiful from October to May on the northern routes. From May until the end of July the number of Common Kittiwakes falls off very rapidly while the breeding birds are at their nesting cliffs. Fewer Common Kittiwakes are likely to be seen on the northern routes at this season, and these are mostly immatures not as yet ready to breed. The number of Northern Fulmars remains almost constant. This may be due to the fact that fulmars may not reach breeding maturity until their seventh year leaving a larger margin of non-breeders at sea.

On the more southern route to New York however, it is the Common Kittiwakes that predominate during the winter and early spring. Later in the summer sometimes a day will pass without a Common Kittiwake being seen and during the latter half of the passage Northern Fulmars disappear at all seasons.

SKUAS. Apart from the above two species, perhaps the most conspicuous and easily identified bird to be seen at any point on all three routes is the **Great Skua (26)**. This large rather heavily built brown bird showing pale flashes on its broad wings often picks up a ship and follows astern for a considerable time watching for galley refuse to appear in the wake. Although, as will be seen, it is more numerous during its migratory passages, it has been seen at sea at all seasons.

Three other smaller skuas or jaegers, the **Pomarine, Arctic** and **Long-tailed Skuas (26)**, cross the three routes during seasonal migrations. Reported observations tend to show that the passage of the skuas is greater in both the eastern and western quarters of the Atlantic. Moreover Pomarine and certainly Long-tailed Skuas are seen more frequently in the western quarter, while Great Skuas, Arctic Skuas and some Pomarine Skuas predominate in the eastern quarter. The main northerly migration appears to cross the routes during late April/May and terminates by mid-June, while the main southerly passage crosses the routes between mid-September and late October.

Compared with the Great Skua, the three smaller skuas appear slender, even hawk-like in build, with narrow wings and swift direct flight. The Pomarine and Arctic Skuas may be seen in either a pale or dark phase plumage, adults in the pale phase showing brown upperparts, straw-coloured necks, dark crowns and pale underparts. The Long-tailed Skua occurs only in the pale phase. In the dark phase the Pomarine and Arctic Skuas are generally dark overall. In adult plumage, except when in moult, the best clue to their identity is the character of their protruding central tail feathers, although the long central points of the Long-tailed Skua are self-evident.

STORM-PETRELS. Three different dark storm-petrels may be seen on all three routes, but only the **British** and **Leach's Storm-petrels (13)** have been recorded at all seasons. The movements of **Wilson's Storm-petrel (13)** are discussed later.

All three are similar at first glance; outstandingly small, sooty-black above with sooty-brown underparts, partly white under tail-coverts and with white patches above the rump. The finer points in plumage and flight characteristics must be looked for to identify them separately.

The British Storm-petrel breeds only along the eastern seaboard of the N. Atlantic and does not appear to spread much beyond 30°W. along the routes. Leach's Storm-petrel on the other hand breeds on both sides of the N. Atlantic. West of 30°W. Leach's Storm-petrel, although it may be seen earlier, usually replaces the British Storm-petrel. Neither are seen regularly, but Leach's predominates.

GULLS. Gulls are seen very rarely in the open oceans during a direct sea passage. In exceptional weather conditions when strong continuous easterly winds have been sweeping across the British Isles, ships have reported the most inshore Common Gulls and Black-headed Gulls driven far out from land. Where Ocean Weather Ships are stationed continuously or fishing trawlers are operating, the larger Herring, Lesser Black-backed, Glaucous and Iceland Gulls collect in small numbers in the northern areas. One exception is the **Great Black-backed Gull (27, 34, 40)** for during winter months it has been observed at all points on the routes, sometimes appearing astern of a ship for one or two consecutive days.

Shearwaters and petrels common to all three routes during periods of seasonal migration

Two shearwaters, the **Great Shearwater (9)** and the **Sooty Shearwater (8)**, and one storm-petrel, **Wilson's Storm-petrel (13)**, spread across the three routes during the early summer and autumn during their great migratory invasion into the N. Atlantic from their breeding quarters far south on the south Atlantic and sub-antarctic islands.

Great Shearwaters and Wilson's Storm-petrels have been observed sweeping northwards in early May some 500 miles east of the W. Indies, heading on a direct course for the Newfoundland Grand Banks.

During May and June, but the northward migration extends beyond these dates, Great Shearwaters and Wilson's Storm-petrels may well be seen in flocks, more particularly the storm-petrels, sweeping in close to the N. American coast off New York and assembling at their favourite feeding area off the Grand Banks where a number remain until October. As summer advances many Great Shearwaters sweep in a wide clockwise circuit following the Westerly Drift, and by late summer, from September onwards numbers appear amongst the British Ocean Weather Ships in the region of 56°N. in the eastern quarter of the northern routes moving southwards. It appears that Wilson's Storm-petrels do not penetrate so far north and separate more widely across the ocean, but it has been established that considerable numbers are to be seen east of 20°W. between August and the end of October on their return passage to the S. Atlantic.

The Sooty Shearwater is also a summer visitor following a migratory route somewhat similar to the Great Shearwater, but apparently on a broader front, occurring in much smaller numbers and usually observed at sea infrequently and only singly or in pairs. It has been seen in the autumn west of Ireland and again near the coasts of N. America and Canada in the early summer.

The larger Great Shearwater with its pale brown upperparts, dusky-white underparts, conspicuously 'dark-capped' appearance and easy sustained shearwatering flight in the Atlantic wind can be distinguished quickly. The smaller stockier Sooty Shearwater, with dusky-black upperparts and greyish-brown underbody, shows a silvery central lining to its underwings, and has not the easy mastery of the Great Shearwater's flight. Its flight is swifter with quick wing-beats and shorter glides on stiff angled wings. The Wilson's Storm-petrel regularly follows ships, fluttering in the wake and dropping its long legs to patter on the surface. It may be distinguished from the rather larger browner and fork-tailed Leach's Storm-petrel, which flies freely and buoyantly paying little immediate attention to ships.

Additional seabirds likely to be seen on sea routes to Canada

AUKS. Common Guillemots have been seen well out in the open ocean and have been recorded on several occasions at all seasons as far as 20°W. The occurrence of Razorbills remains doubtful, for under conditions of 'wave and weather' normal on these northern routes identification is difficult.

The Atlantic Puffin has only been recorded once far out at sea on the route in the eastern N. Atlantic, one having been washed on board, and identified at 15°W. Further north however it has been observed frequently in the open ocean. All three species however become plentiful off the Newfoundland seaboard and in the vicinity of the Flemish Cap where a lookout should also be kept for **Brunnich's Guillemot (46)**. It occurs along the western seaboard of the N. Atlantic and is likely to be seen anywhere from the vicinity of the Grand Banks to the Gulf of St Lawrence. It is very difficult to distinguish at sea from the Common Guillemot, the chief distinguishing feature being its shorter stouter pointed bill with a narrow pale line along the sides. In winter, the dark plumage of the sides of the face extends below the eyes.

On the northern route to the Belle Isle Strait, **Little Auks (46)** are plentiful, sometimes seen west of 30°W. and in large flocks west of 45°W. They are easily recognised by their small stumpy size, rapid wing-beats and habit of disappearing below the surface and reappearing like jack-in-the-boxes.

GULLS. Approaching the coasts of Newfoundland and Nova Scotia, gulls will appear again. The Common Kittiwake, which will have been seen throughout the passage, may be joined by Herring Gulls and the occasional Great Black-backed

Gull. A lookout should be kept for two new species, the **Glaucous Gull (29, 35, 40)** and the **Iceland Gull (29, 33, 35, 40)**. Both species which breed within the Arctic Circle disperse southwards in the autumn and have been seen most frequently in the Belle Isle Strait, but also off the Grand Banks and south as far as New York. When seen separately the two gulls are easily confused for in adult plumage both are 'white-winged' gulls, but the Glaucous Gull is larger and more heavily built, nearing the size of the Great Black-backed Gull. A lookout should also be kept in the region of the Belle Isle Strait for **Kumlien's Gull (p. 100)**, similar to the Iceland Gull but showing grey wing tips.

Thayer's Gull (28, 35), which breeds in arctic Canada, may also occur in this area occasionally.

Gulf of St Lawrence

While Northern Fulmars are to be seen in the open sea in large numbers, increasing in the autumn and winter, it appears that they only enter the Belle Isle Strait in any numbers during July. Within the Gulf of St Lawrence, Northern Fulmars appear in winter months, although small numbers have been recorded in summer months. They are more likely to be seen by ships entering through the Cabot Straits from November onwards.

Within the Gulf itself, a variety of offshore and inshore seabirds may be seen including Great Black-backed and Herring Gulls, and close inshore in the summer months **Ring-billed Gulls (28, 35, 40)**. Brunnich's and Common Guillemots, Razorbills, Atlantic Puffins and Black Guillemots occur, and Northern Gannets which breed on Bird Rock are frequently seen in the Cabot Strait. Common, Arctic and Caspian Terns all breed inland and may be seen up the St Lawrence River.

The route to New York

The route to New York will deprive the observer, except in rare instances in winter months, of opportunities to see Brunnich's Guillemots, Little Auks, Glaucous and Iceland Gulls. In other respects the seabirds already described may be seen.

In the western quarter of the Atlantic route between 60°W. and New York, the four species of skua pass during migration. Common and Arctic Terns, and no doubt other species of tern, follow migration routes in this zone, but difficulty in identification at sea has provided little positive information. In the late autumn Northern Gannets have been observed in small flocks off Sandy Hook, and **Bonaparte's Gulls (31, 36)** moving southwards no doubt to winter off the coasts of Mexico.

This area is also a northwards and southwards passage route for both **Red-necked** and **Grey Phalaropes (25)**, to be seen in flocks, short distances to seaward. Great Shearwaters, Sooty Shearwaters and Wilson's Storm-petrels, referred to earlier, are all likely to be seen at the appropriate seasons.

Approaching harbour Herring and Great Black-backed Gulls will be seen at all seasons and less common Ring-billed Gulls and **Laughing Gulls (31, 36)**.

Eastern Seaboard of the U.S.A.: New York to Houston, Texas

General

The eastern seaboard of the U.S.A. is characterised as a migration route for the northward and southward spring and autumn passages of a number of oceanic seabirds.

Southbound coastal shipping will admittedly pass to the west of the main northward migration of **Great Shearwaters (9)**, **Wilson's Storm-petrels (13)** and the lesser numbers of **Sooty Shearwaters (8)** which stream northwards in the months of

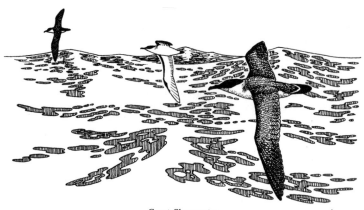

Great Shearwater

May and June towards feeding grounds off the Newfoundland Grand Banks. Nevertheless a voyager leaving New York at this season may not be disappointed, for large flocks of Great Shearwaters and Wilson's Storm-petrels have been observed by ships at no great distance off the Ambrose Light, and some may even be seen by a ship on the sea route south in May or June nearer to the coast. Sooty Shearwaters are more elusive and appear to be scattered more thinly across the N. Atlantic. By the end of July the main movement will have passed further north.

It may be well to direct the attention of the voyager for a moment to the other species of storm-petrel which ranges widely across the Atlantic. **Leach's Storm-petrel (13)**, which breeds off the coasts of Maine and Massachusetts, ranges into the area at all seasons; thus whenever a small dark white-rumped storm-petrel is seen there is always the possibility that identification may be at fault. Wilson's Storm-petrel with its square white rump patch, square tail and weaker gliding and pattering flight is a regular ship follower. Leach's Storm-petrel, somewhat larger and browner in appearance, flies with a buoyant free bounding flight taking little notice of ships; except at the closest range however, the dark feathers dividing its more oval white rump patch and its forked tail will hardly be observed.

Another shearwater, **Cory's Shearwater (9)**, may occur on the sea route, more probably during the summer or autumn. It is more oceanic than coastal, and unlikely to be seen south of the latitude of N. Carolina from shipping records. Both the Great and Cory's Shearwaters are generally similar in size and appearance, medium-large brown birds with whitish underparts and typical 'shearwatering' flight. A noticeable feature in the Great Shearwater is its 'dark capped' appearance set off by a whitish neck and dark bill, while Cory's lacks the distinctive dark cap and has a noticeable rather large yellow bill. Both species show a whitish band above the base of the tail, more pronounced however in the Great Shearwater.

Other migrating oceanic seabirds travel closer to the coast. During May and June, and again in October and November, exact dates always being open to some latitude, **Pomarine**, **Long-tailed**, **Arctic**, and more rarely **Great Skuas (26)** have all been observed on the sea route, usually passing singly or in pairs. Great Skuas have a habit of picking up ships and following astern for considerable periods, Pomarine Skuas occasionally following for shorter periods. Arctic and Long-tailed Skuas pay no attention to ships.

Red-necked Phalaropes (25), which breed in arctic regions and in Labrador, have the habit of collecting in great numbers in the Bay of Fundy in August, thence migrating southwards along the coast of U.S.A. together with **Grey Phalaropes (25)**. Both these dainty little waders are so similar in winter plumage as to be virtually indistinguishable when observed at sea. They will perhaps be first noticed in small flocks resting on the water or taking short rapid flights similar, as one writer quotes, at first sight to sanderlings. Both species have been recorded by ships in spring and autumn along the route as far south as Florida.

There are yet other seabirds which breed in arctic regions such as the **Glaucous Gull (29, 35, 40)** and less commonly the **Iceland Gull (29, 33, 35, 40)** and **Little Auk (46)** which wander southwards in winter months and have been observed by ships at sea occasionally off New York. They rarely extend further south. The pale cream-coloured Glaucous and Iceland Gulls, neither of which show any black wing quills, are very similar in general appearance. When observed together the Glaucous Gull is seen to be considerably larger, nearing the size of the Great Black-backed Gull, while the Iceland Gull is similar in size to a Herring Gull. When mingling with other gulls their pale colouring both in adults and immatures is observable at once.

Common Kittiwakes (33, 39), **Common** and **Brunnich's Guillemots (46)**, **Atlantic Puffins (47)** and **Razorbills (46)** do not breed south of the Gulf of St Lawrence, and the Little Auk in the arctic. They have been reported occasionally east of New York in the winter. Positive identification at sea of the different species of auks is often difficult.

The **Northern Gannet (18)**, which breeds in the Gulf of St Lawrence, disperses considerably further south in winter. Both adults in their white plumage and black primaries, and immatures in speckled brown dress occur regularly off New York; on a few occasions they have been noticed on the coastal route almost as far south as Florida.

Leaving New York

As a ship leaves the harbour, **Herring Gulls (28, 35, 40)** are likely to crowd astern, mingling with **Ring-billed Gulls (28, 35, 40)**. A lone **Great Black-backed Gull (27, 34, 40)** may be seen at a distance. Adult Herring and Ring-billed Gulls are very similar but the Ring-billed Gull is smaller, has a more buoyant flight, shows more black on the underside of the primaries, a conspicuous sub-terminal black band on the bill and greenish-yellow bill and legs. Immatures in speckled brown plumage are harder to tell apart, for the immature Herring Gull shows a black band at the end of the bill at this stage and a broad black band at the base of the tail. Immature Ring-billed Gulls show a thin white band at the base of the tail and a much narrower sub-terminal black band. Both species will follow ships for considerable periods along a coastal route. Early in the southward passage **Laughing Gulls (31, 36)** may appear. Laughing Gulls with their leaden-grey mantle and upperwings, white underparts and blackish-grey 'hoods' in summer plumage are easily identified, a conspicuous white border to the trailing edge of the wings showing in flight.

Before reaching the latitude of Cape Hatteras, and thence southwards, a lookout should be kept for **Audubon's Shearwater (9)**. Audubon's Shearwater, which breeds in the Bahamas and other islands in the W. Indies, ranges northwards along the southern east coast of the U.S.A. and has been observed frequently as far north as Cape Hatteras. It appears as a small sturdy shearwater with rich brown upperparts, palish underwings, white cheeks and underbody and dark under tail-coverts. It flies with a short series of rapid wing-beats and glides, often occurring in flocks wheeling over the sea, settling and diving readily.

Cape Hatteras towards Grand Bahama Island

From now onwards the route will diverge from the coast outside the normal range of the gulls. Few seabirds are likely to be seen apart from the occasional sighting of Audubon's Shearwater, and, during the spring and autumn, the chance sighting of a passing skua or flock of phalaropes.

TERNS. Along the low-lying shores and inlets which comprise much of the east coast of the U.S.A., many terns breed but they rarely extend to the sea routes and are even less certainly identified from ships at sea. Those seen pass by quickly giving little opportunity against a background of sea or sky to verify their species. One tern, however, the **Sooty Tern (44)**, ranges widely over the ocean and occasionally these handsome terns have been seen well out at sea off the coast of Florida. Superficially they are easily recognised by their blackish-brown crown, upperparts and deeply forked tail, white forehead and whitish underparts, a white piping showing to the outer tail feathers in flight. At sea however, they may be confused with the very similar **Brown-winged** or **Bridled Tern (44)** which is more likely to be seen further south off Florida and beyond. On first sighting it is well to study the detailed descriptions of each species.

The Straits of Florida

As the route passes between Great Bahama I. and the southern coast of Florida, the number and variety of seabirds will increase rapidly. Not all which are mentioned are likely to be seen in the course of one sea passage; most, if not all, however may be seen at all seasons of the year.

Magnificent Frigate-bird

On the sandy spits of the Bahamas many terns breed – the **Common Tern (42, 43)**, the **Sandwich Tern (41, 43)**, the **Roseate Tern (42)**, the **Royal Tern (41)** and the **Little** and **Gull-billed Terns (43)**, the latter very much an 'inshore tern'. Hard by in the mangrove swamps, **Magnificent Frigate-birds (24)**, **Brown Pelicans (17)**, **Brown Boobies (19)**, **Blue-faced Boobies (18)** and **Double-crested Cormorants (21)** are a common sight.

Great colonies of Sooty Terns and **Common Noddies (44)** breed on the low-lying coral islands of the Dry Tortugas west of Key West. Many Sooty Terns have been banded on these islands and some idea of the remarkable oceanic journeyings of these birds may be illustrated by recoveries of banded birds having occurred across the full breadth of the Atlantic in Ghana, Nigeria and elsewhere. Brown-winged or Bridled Terns also breed widely throughout the W. Indies and the possibility of sighting this species may also occur.

In this area too, during November and through January, Pomarine Skuas, which winter in considerable numbers in the Caribbean, are very likely to be seen. Ships have reported seeing Pomarine Skuas joining the Magnificent Frigate-birds harrying boobies and other seabirds at these seasons.

The Straits of Florida to Houston

Crossing the Gulf of Mexico the ship will be outside the range of the Laughing Gulls, Ring-billed Gulls and those Herring Gulls which winter on the coasts of Louisiana. Sooty Terns have been seen occasionally and there are records of Audubon's Shearwaters in the eastern portion of the Gulf, but seabirds are likely to be few and far between. On approaching Galveston, Laughing Gulls, Ring-billed Gulls and **American White Pelicans (17)** are likely to appear again and many varieties of terns.

British Isles to the Caribbean

A considerable part of the ocean route towards the W. Indies offers few opportunities to the birdwatcher for the number and variety of oceanic seabirds are limited.

Nevertheless many of the seabirds quoted have been recorded during a single passage, the areas to the north and north-west of the Azores and on approaching and passing the W. Indian Is. being particularly favourable.

The outset of the passage through the English Channel is described in Route 9.

From the English Channel to the Azores

Herring Gulls (28, 35, 40) and **Lesser Black-backed Gulls (27, 35, 40)** sometimes continue to follow ships well out of sight of land, and the **Northern Gannet (18)** has been observed in the open ocean beyond the limits of the continental shelf.

The sea route to the Panama Canal passes some 300 miles to the north-west of the Azores. Although yellow-legged Herring Gulls, Common and Roseate Terns breed on the islands, and **Great Black-backed Gulls (27, 34, 40)** are winter visitors, none of these will be seen so far out at sea.

On reaching the open sea from the English Channel the **Common Kittiwake (33, 39)**, **Northern Fulmar (11)**, **Manx Shearwater (9)** and **British Storm-petrel (13)** are those most likely to be seen at the outset. Common Kittiwakes have been seen frequently by ships as far as the longitude of the Azores. Numbers increase during the autumn and winter months, but from June until the autumn few will be seen,

Sooty Shearwater

34

breeding adults being at their nesting quarters to the north, those remaining at sea being mostly immatures or non-breeders, the immatures in their distinctive plumage.

The route passes quickly south of the normal oceanic range of the Northern Fulmar but one or two have been seen occasionally as far as 30°W. The Manx Shearwater, which breeds during the early summer both in the British Isles and the Azores, does not wander far from the land during the breeding season and has been recorded only rarely well out in the ocean.

Three other shearwaters are liable to be seen between the British Isles and the longitude of the Azores, the **Sooty Shearwater (8)**, and the **Great** and **Cory's Shearwaters (9)**.

Cory's Shearwater

Numerically the Cory's Shearwater is likely to be seen most often. It breeds on the Azores from May to September and is likely to be seen at all seasons but to a lesser extent from December to April. Both the Great and Sooty Shearwaters are summer migrants to the N. Atlantic, the greatest numbers passing northwards in the western quarter of the N. Atlantic between late April and early June, sweeping in a clockwise circuit during the southward return to the far S. Atlantic, passing across the route at this stage of the passage between September and November.

STORM-PETRELS. The British Storm-petrel breeds in considerable numbers on the west coasts of the British Isles and **Leach's Storm-petrel (13)** in smaller numbers. Leach's Storm-petrel spreads right across the N. Atlantic and is certainly seen more frequently than **Wilson's Storm-petrel (13)**; it may be seen at all seasons. Wilson's, on the other hand, undertakes a very similar migration route to the two migrant shearwaters, and is most likely to be seen at this stage on the route in the autumn. The **Madeiran Storm-petrel (13)** breeds on the Azores but is unlikely to be seen far to seawards. Throughout the mid-ocean passage it is Leach's Storm-petrel that predominates. Somewhat larger and browner in appearance than Wilson's, it flies freely clear of ships, while Wilson's is a regular ship follower, flitting from side to side in the wake, often dropping its long legs to the surface while picking up food.

SKUAS. Of the four migratory skuas, it is the **Great** and **Pomarine Skuas (26)** that occasionally pick up a ship during their northerly and southerly migrations in April/May and September/October. The large brown Great Skua with its pale wing patches often follow ships for considerable periods; the smaller Pomarine Skua with its more hawk-like flight and slightly protruding twisted central tail feathers pays but a passing interest.

The sea area north of the Azores

The observations of many sea passages along the route have shown a marked concentration principally of Cory's and Great Shearwaters and to a lesser extent of Leach's Storm-petrels in the sea area enclosed between 20° to 40°W. and 50° to 40°N. In general Cory's Shearwaters appear to be more prevalent at sea between July and November. It is now clear from many records that numbers disperse southwards from the area of the eastern Atlantic islands from November onwards, many birds wintering off the west Coast of S. Africa, others dispersing westwards towards the American coast. The Great Shearwaters are more prevalent in the Azores area between September and November after which they move southwards. Sooty Shearwaters are also occasionally seen singly in the area at similar seasons, and on rarer occasions Manx Shearwaters.

Southwards from the Azores

Beyond the 'Azores sea area' to some 400 miles north-east of the Leeward Is. the route covers a particularly birdless part of the ocean. Days may pass without a seabird being sighted, the only creatures on the 'fin' being flying fishes. During this somewhat barren period of the voyage, Leach's Storm-petrels may be seen if a sharp lookout is kept, and during the spring, late summer and autumn the chance sighting of a passing skua, Great Shearwater, Manx Shearwater and Wilson's Storm-petrel.

Approaching the West Indian islands

During the spring and at the peak periods of May and early June Great Shearwaters and Wilson's Storm-petrels are streaming northwards on a flypath some 500 miles to the north-east of the islands on a migration route which will bring them to rich feeding areas off the Newfoundland Grand Banks. The occasional Great Skua, Pomarine Skua and **Long-tailed Skua (26)** may be sighted similarly northward bound. As the ship continues to close the islands the more oceanic tropical seabirds will begin to appear. The first of these are likely to be **Sooty Terns (44)**, **Red-billed** and **White-tailed Tropic-birds (15)**, appearing as scouts to welcome the ship. The white tropic-birds with their long streaming central tail feathers flying with strong wing-beats, usually at a considerable height, are very noticeable, and the dark-backed Sooty Tern with white underparts gives a floating buoyant appearance in flight.

Upwelling water off the eastern shores of the islands provides a natural feeding ground for offshore tropical seabirds, and boobies may be the next species to be seen. Flocks of **Brown Boobies (19)**, the most numerous of the three species common to the W. Indies, have been seen over 200 miles from the islands but this is perhaps exceptional. The boobies are of the same family as the Northern Gannet and possess the same general characteristics in form and flight. The Brown Booby in adult plumage is unmistakable with its dark chocolate-brown head, neck, breast and upperparts, showing a clear cut line between its dark breast and white underparts.

Two other boobies to be looked for are the **Blue-faced Booby (18)** and the **Red-footed Booby (19)**.

Before penetrating the islands an observer may see a small sturdy shearwater, sometimes in flocks, with rich dark brown upperparts and white underparts flying with a rapid flutter of several wing-beats and short glides over the sea. More than likely this will be **Audubon's Shearwater (9)**, common within the islands.

Passing between the islands

A great variety of tropical seabirds live amongst the islands, but from a ship passing through on a single voyage the list of those seen and identified is sure to be far from complete. Not all are quoted but those most commonly seen deserve special mention. The boobies may be seen at any time. Close around harbours and coastlines the **Brown Pelican (17)** will be unmistakable, and here too the **Magnificent Frigate-bird (24)**, the only species of frigate-bird in this area, will almost certainly be seen. This large dark long-winged bird, known as the 'Man o'War Hawk' by seamen, circles overhead looking for opportunities to chivvy boobies and other seabirds and make them disgorge their pickings.

Flying here and there between the islands Sooty Terns, the browner-coloured but very similar **Brown-winged** or **Bridled Terns (44)**, and the dark brown **Common Noddy (44)**, with its pale, almost white crown, are all likely to be seen.

Common, Roseate and Little Terns all breed on the islands but are not identified often by ships. These and other terns which winter in the islands are not amongst the normal run of sightings, but the **Royal Tern (41)** is certainly more likely to catch the eye. It is a large handsome tern in the usual grey and white pattern but with elongated feathers on its black crown and a stout distinctive red bill.

The **Laughing Gull (31, 36)**, which breeds on the islands, is the only gull almost certainly to be seen close round harbours and bays. It is common and plentiful from March throughout the summer, but many migrate further south during the winter.

The central Caribbean

In this area at a distance from the islands and mainland, seabirds become distinctly scarcer, and those most likely to be seen will be Sooty Terns, Red-billed Tropic-birds and an occasional Common Noddy. Audubon's Shearwaters have also been seen occasionally. A lookout should also be kept for the much rarer **Black-capped Petrel (10)**, known to breed only on Hispaniola.

There is however one exception during the winter months, usually from late November to January when Pomarine Skuas appear in considerable numbers and must clearly use the Caribbean as one wintering area.

The ship may be bound onward to the Panama Canal where seabirds to be seen are described in Route 20. Further details of seabirds within the Caribbean zone will be found in Route 4.

ROUTE 6

British Isles to East Coasts of Brazil and Uruguay via Cape Verde Islands

The early part of this route passes down the English Channel and thence direct to the Cape Verde Is. The voyager will find the seabirds which occur up to this point in Route 9 and the first part of Route 7.

Thereafter the passage continues across the warm tropical belt of the Atlantic to the vicinity of St Paul's Rocks at the Equator, whose craggy wave-washed tops emerge abruptly from the depths of the mid-Atlantic ridge, and whose sole occupants are **Brown Boobies (19)** and **Common** and **White-capped Noddies (44)**. Ahead

Brown Booby passing old beacon of St Paul's Rocks

along the route lies the island of Fernando de Noronha, off the bulge of Brazil, whose phonolite peak sticks up like a jagged tooth. The route continues towards a landfall off Cape Frio and so coastwise to Rio de Janeiro and Buenos Aires.

Southwards from the Cape Verde Is. the mid-Atlantic is notable for its lack of seabird life. A chance sighting of a **Little Shearwater (9)** a **Red-billed Tropic-bird (15)**, a **Pomarine Skua (26)** passing on migration in April or October, **Bulwer's Petrel (9)** and later perhaps the occasional **Sooty Tern (44)** may occur. Some Sooty Terns are now known to disperse rather unaccountably from the direction of the Florida Keys towards the Gulf of Guinea in the autumn. **Leach's Storm-petrel (13)**, that great wanderer over the breadth of the Atlantic, has been reported most frequently however, although only in ones or twos at long intervals. A keen lookout is needed

38

Red-billed Tropicbird

to pick up this little dark storm-petrel over the wide expanse of ocean. Recently however, during a passage in December, **Bulwer's Petrel** was identified at intervals between the Cape Verde Is. and St Paul's Rocks. This very small sooty-brown petrel may be distinguished by its long wedge-shaped tail.

It is not until approaching St Paul's Rocks that seabird life begins to increase. Brown Boobies, these large brown tropical gannets showing a brown breast sharply divided from white underparts in adult plumage, tend to range further to seaward than the Common Noddies and White-capped Noddies which breed on the Rocks. From now onwards seabirds are likely to become more frequent. Large numbers of **Red-footed Boobies (19)** colonise Fernando de Noronha I., while **Red-billed** and **White-tailed Tropic-birds (15)**, **Sooty Terns (44)** and **Magnificent Frigate-birds (24)** also nest on the island. Sooty Terns, tropic-birds and Red-footed Boobies range widely across the oceans but at sea it is always a difficult matter to differentiate between the two species of tropic-birds. It is not unusual for tropic-birds and less commonly Sooty Terns to follow in the wake of ships at night, attracted no doubt by squids thrown up by the propellors, for both species feed largely on squid. Their strident calls usually give the first indication of their presence. Red-footed Boobies sometimes settle on ships at sea, using ships' davits or the forecastle rails as a perch from which to pursue flying fish disturbed from the bow wake.

The coast of northern Brazil

In addition to the seabirds already quoted **Blue-faced Boobies (18)** may be seen.

The sea area off the bulge of Brazil is also one through which **Great Shearwaters (9)**, **Sooty Shearwaters (8)** and **Wilson's Storm-petrels (13)** pass during their northward spring migrations into the westward quarter of the N. Atlantic. Between April and May these species are almost certain to be seen, often quite close to the coast all the way south to Buenos Aires. They occur again from October onwards moving southwards.

A further shearwater, **Audubon's Shearwater (9)**, which breeds on islands along the north-east coast of S. America, has been seen by ships on occasions round the bulge of Brazil. Audubon's Shearwater is very similar in appearance to the **Manx Shearwater (9)** which has also been reported as a migrant from the British Isles and the eastern Atlantic islands in winter months. Audubon's is however browner in appearance, has a longer tail with black under tail-coverts and flies with stiffer faster wing-beats between glides. At sea these points are difficult to observe unless the two species are seen together, an unlikely event for neither are common in the area. **Brown Boobies** and **Magnificent Frigate-birds** may be seen frequently on the coast of Brazil.

As the ship proceeds southwards species common in the southern oceans will begin to appear. During the southern winter (June to October) many have tended to move northwards.

The southern **Great Skua (26)** migrates northwards from the sub-antarctic zone, and from April onwards numbers are seen at sea at no distance from the coast. At this season too albatrosses, Pintado Petrels and prions will begin to be seen from about 25°S.

The first albatross more likely than not will be the **Yellow-nosed Albatross (5)**. The first sight of an albatross accompanying a ship always evokes interest and there should be little difficulty in differentiating this smaller and slenderer albatross from the large Wandering Albatross. In the adult Yellow-nosed Albatross one should look for its sooty-black back, dark brownish-black upperwings, broad white underwing linings with thin black edges terminating in a black triangle, and particularly for its black bill carrying a bright yellow line along its upper ridge and an orange tip. The **Pintado Petrel (11)**, the commonest and most strikingly coloured piebald petrel of the southern oceans, is quite unmistakable. Flocks regularly collect and follow ships, and will increase in numbers as the ship continues south. The little **prions (11)**, there are in all six separate species, indistinguishable at sea, have blue-grey upperparts with a darker W pattern across the wings, white underparts and black tips to their wedge-shaped tails. They usually occur in flocks, banking and twisting in unison in rapid flight.

The **Wandering Albatross (3)** is usually seen a little further south than the Yellow-nosed Albatross. With its very large size, extremely long narrow wings, dignified and majestic flight, peaked crown and humped back, it outclasses the smaller albatrosses, but it must be borne in mind that more often than not it will be seen in one of the many variations of immature plumage.

The Wandering Albatross is greatly attached to ships and accompanies them more persistently than all others. With the arrival of the 'Wanderer', the **Black-browed Albatross (5)** is also likely to appear and might be confused with the Yellow-nosed Albatross on first acquaintance as its adult plumage is very similar. A look at its yellow bill and the wider blurred black edges to its underwings and thick 'neckless' hump-backed appearance will help to identify it.

Further south still, three new oceanic petrels are likely to be seen of which the commonest and a regular ship follower is the **White-chinned Petrel (7).** This is a very large sooty-black petrel with a massive pale bill and a white area under the chin, sometimes extending round the face. It follows astern with an easy flapping and gliding flight. **Manx Shearwaters** may also be seen in November and December.

Here too the large and quite unmistakable **Giant Petrel (6, 7)** may join with others on the lookout for garbage thrown overboard. This massive grey-brown petrel, the size of a small albatross with narrow wings, great straw-coloured bill and stiff winged flapping flight is an unpleasant customer, gobbling up young penguins at their breeding colonies and happily feeding on all manner of carrion.

Approaching Buenos Aires a lookout should be kept for **Schlegel's Petrel (10)**, a species regularly seen in the southern quarter of the S. Atlantic by ships on passage from the Cape of Good Hope to Buenos Aires

GULLS. Gulls are rarely seen offshore, and in ports north of Santos little detail is available from ships. Further south however the commonest gull to be seen in harbours is the **Southern Black-backed Gull (27, 34, 40)**, the counterpart of the Lesser Black-backed Gull of northern waters. It is the only large black-backed gull in the southern hemisphere with a pale white tail in adult plumage. The **Patagonian Black-headed Gull (31, 36)** is hard to distinguish in adult plumage from the Northern Black-headed Gull. The **Grey-headed Gull (30, 36, 38)** is rather larger than the Patagonian Black-headed Gull, and in adult summer plumage has a lavender-grey head and throat.

TERNS. The usual difficulty of identifying terns always arises. South of Rio de Janeiro, if terns having the appearance of Common or Arctic Terns are seen, they will probably be **South American Terns (42)**. These breed along the coast of S. America as far as Tierra del Fuego and have frequently been observed.

PENGUINS. The **Magellan Penguin (1)** occurs at sea, often close off the coast, and has been seen as far north as Santos, but this is probably exceptional. It usually collects in small parties, swims low in the water but holds its head high with bill often tilted upwards. They breed from the Falkland Is. southward to Cape Horn and like other oceanic species follow the cold Falkland Current northwards.

British Isles to Cape Town

Until Cape Finisterre is passed the seabirds have been described in Route 9. Thereafter the sea route diverges from the coast of Portugal passing east of Madeira.

As Cape Finisterre is left behind, inshore seabirds will soon disappear and the ship will soon be passing beyond the southern zone of the Common Kittiwakes. At the outset a Great Skua or a Northern Gannet may be seen but it will be the Cory's Shearwater, Manx Shearwater and British Storm-petrel that are more likely to cross the ship's path. From October through November however, both the Great Shearwater and Wilson's Storm-petrel begin to appear in the area; they have already commenced their return journeys from their spring and summer migratory invasions into the N. Atlantic, and will be on their way back to breeding quarters at the Tristan da Cunha Is. and sub-antarctic islands respectively. The 'dark-capped' appearance and slender dark bill of the Great Shearwater will help to distinguish it from Cory's Shearwater which, though otherwise very similar, lacks the 'dark-capped' aspect and has a stout yellow bill noticeable at some distance.

The ship will pass Madeira at too great a distance for the gulls and terns which breed there to appear. Cory's and Manx Shearwaters and three species not appearing in Route 9 also breed at Madeira –the **Little Shearwater (9)**, **Bulwer's Petrel (9)** and the **Madeiran Storm-petrel (13)**.

The Little Shearwater although very similar in plumage appearance to the Manx Shearwater is so much smaller and flies with such rapid wing-beats in comparison to the more masterly shearwatering of the Manx that it should not be difficult to

White-faced Storm-petrel

identify. Bulwer's Petrel is equally small but its overall dark plumage, distinctly long wedge-shaped tail and undulating flight low over the sea will distinguish it from storm-petrels. The Madeiran Storm-petrel on the other hand is so much like the British and Wilson's Storm-petrels that it is frequently mistaken at sea. It is usually seen singly and normally does not follow ships.

The route will pass close to the Salvage Is. where the majority of these oceanic species breed. Here too the **White-faced Storm-petrel (13)** breeds. It has been reported frequently, partly no doubt on account of its distinctive plumage, for the grey portions of its upperparts, its white face, dark eye patch, white underparts and fast zigzag flight distinguish it from other dark storm-petrels.

Approaching the Canary Islands

The peak of Mount Teide (12,163 ft) on Tenerife can be seen above the horizon from the bridge of a ship sometimes at 80 miles distance, for this is a sea area where light winds and fair weather normally prevail. The oceanic 'tubenoses' already mentioned may all be seen on occasion, and when passing through the islands inshore gulls may appear.

Common Gulls, yellow-legged Herring Gulls, and the Common and Little Terns are breeding species; Great Black-backed and Lesser Black-backed Gulls and Northern Gannets occur as winter visitors, the latter often in large numbers with immatures.

The bulge of North-west Africa

The ship will now be passing close round the bulge of N.W. Africa, past the Cape Verde Is. as far as Liberia. In this area enclosed roughly between 30° and 10°N. and from the coast to 20°W., enormous numbers of both sea and land birds pass during their seasonal migrations, many also staying to winter. Here the cool south-westerly flowing Canaries Current, deflected away from the land, creates an area of upwelling cool water bringing to the surface nutrient salts, chiefly phosphates and nitrates which propagate an abundance of plankton and a natural feeding ground for seabirds.

Flocks of dainty **Grey Phalaropes (25)** winter in this area. The **Great Skua (26)** and two of the smaller skuas the **Pomarine** and **Arctic Skuas (26)** pass through on migration. The **Long-tailed Skua (26)** has certainly been observed on several occasions, but its ultimate wintering area is uncertain. Pomarine Skuas are seen more frequently, occasionally in small parties, some possibly wintering in the area, others certainly wintering off S. Africa. April and May and again from October onwards are the peak periods. In the autumn and winter months the beautiful **Sabine's Gull (33, 39)** occurs, a passage migrant, to winter off S. Africa from its sub-arctic breeding quarters. Its pure white plumage is set off by a striking upper-wing pattern appearing as three distinct triangles of grey, white and black, and at close quarters its white tail will be seen to be slightly forked.

Terns are seen here, sometimes in abundance, during winter months and in spring before their northward migration. **Common Terns (42, 43)** and **Arctic Terns (41, 42)**, difficult to differentiate at sea, **Roseate (42)** and **Little Terns (43)** are frequent, Sandwich and Caspian Terns in lesser numbers. The most outstanding sight however may be the spectacle, noted on several occasions, of large flocks of **Black Terns (44)**. Numbers again appear to reach a peak during April and May and in

Pomarine and Arctic Skuas

September and October. It is true that it is those ships trading coastwise round the 'Bulge' that get the real opportunities of seeing the visitations of these more coast-loving seabirds; and there are others, such as the **Grey-headed Gull (30, 36, 38)** and **Royal Tern (41)**, which fall outside the scope of the main sea route.

Some new species which are unlikely to have been seen up to this point breed on the Cape Verde Is., for the ship is now well within the zone of tropical seabirds. Here the **Magnificent Frigate-bird (24)**, the **Brown Booby (19)**, the **Red-billed Tropic-bird (15)** and the **Soft-plumaged Petrel (10)** breed between December and March. Experience shows that the first three species are only seen occasionally, but the Soft-plumaged Petrel is not uncommon. The large long-winged black Magnificent Frigate-bird so often seen floating in the sky overhead with its sinister cruelly-hooked bill, or swooping to chivvy some passing seabird is the very opposite to the white Red-billed Tropic-bird flying swiftly past the ship, its long marline spike tail feather streaming behind.

The Brown Booby by its shape and flight places it at once amongst the family of tropical gannets. The Soft-plumaged Petrel might be mistaken for the White-faced Storm-petrel were it not for its considerably larger size, the dark undersurface of its wings and fast twisting flight on angled wings.

Leach's Storm-petrel (13) has not yet been mentioned; it is described in Route 9, and probably ranges more widely across the whole belt of the N. Atlantic than all other dark storm-petrels. It may have been seen already earlier in the passage. The appearance of Wilson's Storm-petrel will not only be confined to the autumn during its return to its breeding areas. It is now clear that numbers move northwards from April onwards following the Benguela Current off the west coast of S. Africa. It seems probable that these birds may continue north-westwards from the bulge of N.W. Africa towards the Newfoundland Banks.

Southwards from Sierra Leone

The route now diverges from the proximity of land well to the west of the Gulf of Guinea and few seabirds are likely to be seen. From here onwards until reaching the southern latitude where the first albatross will be seen, the occasional sighting of a Pomarine Skua, Arctic Skua, Great Skua or **Arctic Tern (41, 42)** on migration may occur. The handsome black and white **Sooty Tern (44)**, which ranges far out over the tropical belts of the oceans, breeds on Sao Tomé in the Gulf of Guinea, Ascension and St Helena Is. Many Sooty Terns appear to concentrate in the Gulf of Guinea area in the autumn, some apparently migrating from the Caribbean area, and these are always likely to be seen. They have a habit of following ships at night when their loud screeching call notes may attract attention. Of the oceanic shearwaters and petrels occasional sightings of Cory's Shearwater may arise in the late autumn for numbers of these certainly cross the Equator into more southerly latitudes during the winter. The Soft-plumaged Petrel, Leach's Storm-petrel and Wilson's Storm-petrel occur on this part of the route, and the British Storm-petrel migrates southwards as far as the Cape of Good Hope. A lookout should also be kept for the **White-bellied Storm-petrel (13)** which disperses northwards, even as far as the Equator during the southern winter and has been seen along the route northwards to about 15°S. occasionally. **Schlegel's Petrel (10)** may also be seen in the area.

Onwards towards Cape Town

At approximately 16°S. the ship will be entering the northern limit of the wintering range of the oceanic seabirds of the southern oceans, and the traveller must turn his thoughts to the months between May and September.

Although still within the tropics, the surface temperature of the sea begins to fall, due to the northward flowing Benguella Current. Many seabirds which breed in the remote southern ocean and sub-antarctic islands move northwards during the southern winter well north of the Tropic of Capricorn. From May to October visiting albatrosses, many of them immature birds, shearwaters and petrels are likely to be seen in increasing numbers. Indeed the first albatross, almost certainly a **Wandering Albatross (3)**, may pick up a ship as far north as 12°S. although this is uncommon. As the ship steams southwards from the Tropic of Capricorn, the number and variety of species will increase rapidly. In addition to the Wandering Albatross, **Black-browed** and **Yellow-nosed Albatrosses (5)** will appear, and the **Shy Albatross (4)**, which unlike the first three tends to keep well clear of ships. A first clue to these magnificent oceanic seabirds may be gained from a study of their upper- and underwing plumage pattern and coloration of their bills. They take many years to assume full adult plumage however and those without experience of albatrosses may not find it easy to differentiate between birds in immature plumage.

Shearwaters and petrels will now begin to appear. Of these the **White-chinned Petrel (7)** will probably be seen quite frequently for it is an inveterate ship follower. This is a large heavily built sooty-black petrel with a massive, greenish-yellow bill and normally showing a distinctive white chin. A smaller medium-sized dark brown petrel, the **Grey-faced Petrel (10)**, with a grey patch around the base of the bill and face, is equally common but does not follow ships.

As the ship approaches 30°S. all the species already mentioned tend to increase. The **Schlegel's Petrel (10)** may occur, and other species which breed far south and reach these latitudes in the non-breeding season in May to October. Somewhat lesser numbers are to be seen however at all seasons.

Apart from those already mentioned regular records have occurred of the **Sooty Albatross (6)**, **Southern Great Skua (26)**, **Giant Petrel (6, 7)**, **Pintado Petrel (11)**, **Sooty Shearwater (8)**, **Great Shearwater (9)**, **White-bellied Storm-petrel (13)**, **prions (11)** and **Schlegel's Petrel (10)**.

Approaching Cape Town

As the ship closes the coast **Cape Gannets (18)** may begin to appear. Colonies breed along the coast of Cape Province and the birds are often seen some distance offshore. Three species of cormorant occur along the coastline, the **Cape**, **Bank** and **White-necked Cormorants (20)**, mentioned although too coast-loving to be seen on the main shipping route. The **Jackass Penguin (1)** breeds on islands off the extreme southern coast of S. Africa.

Table Bay

The first sight of the massif of Table Mountain with its high flat silhouette often shrouded in cloud heralds the final arrival, and in the outer anchorage the ship may be greeted by the sight of **Southern Black-backed Gulls (27, 34, 40)**, the smaller pale grey-backed but otherwise white **Silver Gull**, known locally as **Hartlaub's Gull (29, 38, 40)** with its red bill and legs, and occasionally the delicate **Damara Tern (43)** and the **Crested Tern (41)**. Another tern likely to be seen is the **Caspian Tern (41)**. The **Common Tern (42, 43)**, **Arctic Tern (41, 42)** and **Sandwich Tern (41, 43)** are migrants from the north, but common along the coastlines during the southern summer.

Cape Town to Buenos Aires

The route from Cape Town to Buenos Aires crosses the S. Atlantic between 35° and 40°S approximately, well within the regular belt of albatrosses and other southern ocean shearwaters and petrels. Certain species may be seen regularly throughout the entire crossing, being normally more abundant within the limits of the cool Benguela Current off the west coast of S. Africa and the northward flowing Falkland Current off the east coast of S. America. For once an observer may be able to study identical species day after day.

Within this belt of ocean there is little hard and fast rule as to the particular seasons in which differing species will be present, for although a number of the sub-antarctic breeding species move further north, and even north of the belt during the southern winter, there remain immatures and non-breeders who are present throughout the year. In addition the Tristan da Cunha Is. and Gough I. accommodate a considerable number of breeding oceanic species which tend to spread over the route.

Oceanic species breeding on Tristan da Cunha Islands or Gough Island

Rock-hopper Penguin, Wandering, Yellow-nosed and Sooty Albatrosses; Northern Giant Petrels, White-chinned, Grey-faced, Soft-plumaged, Brown, Kerguelen and Schlegel's Petrels; Great Shearwater and Little Shearwater; White-bellied and Grey-backed Storm-petrels; Southern Skua, Broad-billed Prion and Common Diving-petrel and Antarctic or Wreathed Tern. Rock-hopper Penguins and Common Noddies also breed but are not oceanic by nature.

Pintado and Giant Petrels

The passage

Once clear to seaward from Table Bay one may see **Wandering**, **Yellow-nosed** and **Black-browed Albatrosses (5)** and frequently, but usually keeping well clear of ships, the **Shy Albatross (4)**. In addition the large and ugly **Giant Petrel (6, 7)** will join the great seabirds.

At the outset also the **Grey-faced Petrel (10)**, the **White-chinned Petrel (7)** and **Pintado Petrel (11)** may be seen regularly, the latter two species being persistent ship followers, and the **Southern Great Skua (26)** should be looked out for. **Wilson's Storm-petrel (13)** and **Sooty Shearwaters (8)** have been seen between September and November and may also occur during the early spring.

As the ship proceeds westwards before reaching the longitude of the Tristan da Cunha Is., other species may appear; almost certainly (this is a dangerous word to use!) the **Great Shearwater (9)**, the **Soft-plumaged** and **Schlegel's Petrels (10)** and small **prions (11)**.

Schlegel's Petrel

As the passage proceeds

With so many species already mentioned it may be helpful to list those which from a study of reports may be seen on any day from now onwards with certain reservations:

Wandering and Yellow-nosed Albatrosses: the Shy Albatross has not yet appeared on shipping records west of the longitude of Tristan da Cunha, and the Black-browed Albatross less frequently in mid-ocean.

Pintado Petrels: these attractive piebald petrels often follow ships in flocks.

Schlegel's Petrel: a 'regular' along the route. With its dark brown upperparts, brown throat and foreneck, white underparts and brown underwings, it is usually seen singly or in ones or twos.

Giant Petrel: its dusky grey-brown plumage, very large size, enormous pale bill, and stiff winged flight make it unmistakable.

Great Shearwater and Sooty Shearwater: these are to be seen right across the ocean along the route during the autumn months from October until the end of November and may well be seen in mid-ocean in the early months of the spring. The Sooty Shearwater, with its sooty-brown upperparts, greyish underparts and a distinct pale central lining to its underwings, may be seen low over the sea shearwatering with a few intermittent quick wing-beats. Like the Sooty Shearwater, the Wilson's Storm-petrel may be seen at intervals at similar seasons.

Little is known of the range of the **White-bellied** and **Black-bellied Storm-petrels (13)**. The all dark Wilson's with its square white rump patch is a keen ship follower; these other two species with their white underparts and method of lowering their legs and hopping along the surface when searching for food are distinguishable from Wilson's but the difference between the White-bellied and the indistinct thin dark central dividing line in the Black-bellied birds is difficult to determine at sea. The different species of prions are impossible to identify at sea. They move northwards during the southern winter from their principal breeding areas on islands in the southern ocean, and have been seen between September and November when they are probably moving southwards. These little birds, scarcely larger than starlings, with their blue-grey backs showing a dark W pattern on the upperwing and their pale white underparts are often seen in flocks flying swiftly low over the sea, turning and tilting in their flight.

These then are the seabirds which are most regularly to be seen throughout the main ocean passage. The Soft-plumaged Petrel appears to be confined to the eastern half of the passage. This medium-small petrel can be distinguished from the considerably larger Schlegel's Petrel by its slate-grey back, white face and throat and dark eye patch, dark brown underwings and its fast erratic flight low over the sea.

Approaching the coast of S. America

As a ship approaches the coast the cold northward flowing Falkland Current with its enriched surface feed attracts greater numbers of the oceanic seabirds which have already been seen. A main stream of Great Shearwaters, Sooty Shearwaters and Wilson's Storm-petrels follows the east coast of S. America on their northerly and southerly migration routes to and from the N. Atlantic while the southern Great Skua follows suit, but does not reach the Equator. These three species are most likely to be crossing the route in April and again between October and November when many sightings have occurred along the whole seaboard. There is some uncertainty as to the dividing line between the northerly limit of the southern Great Skua and the southerly limit of the northern Great Skua, for in May and June sightings of Great Skuas have occurred northwards and onwards past the 'bulge' of Brazil. White-chinned Petrels and prions are seen frequently again, prions often in very large flocks. During the winter months a lookout should be kept for the **Manx Shearwater (9)** wintering in the area from its N. Atlantic breeding quarters, but few have been observed.

On nearing the coast **Southern Black-backed Gulls (27, 34, 40)** and **Patagonian Black-headed Gulls (31, 36)** may well come to escort the ship towards the long entrance to the Rio de la Plata. The **Grey-headed Gull (30, 36, 38)** has also been seen in harbour less frequently, resorting more to inland waters. The Southern

Black-backed Gull is the counterpart of the Lesser Black-backed Gull of the northern hemisphere, although of sturdier proportions, while the Patagonian Black-headed Gull could easily be taken for the Northern Black-headed Gull of northern seas.

TERNS. Identification at sea is always difficult. If terns are seen, they will most probably be **South American Terns (42)** which breed on the eastern coast of S. America and are very similar in appearance to both the Arctic and Common Terns.

PENGUINS. It is not an uncommon sight to see small parties of penguins off the east coast of the Argentine during the southern winter. The **Magellan Penguin (1)** and the **Rock-hopper Penguin (2)** both breed in the Falkland Is. and move northwards with the Falkland Current to the latitude of Buenos Aires. Penguins swim low in the water with backs awash and their rather large heads held high, and will 'porpoise' and dive to keep clear of ships. A quick clue as to the identity of these penguins can be gained by observing the head. In the Rock-hopper with its red bill the whole head, sides of the face, chin and throat are slaty-black and a line of yellow plumes may be seen running back from the bill to above the eye. In the Magellan Penguin a narrow white band runs along the sides and crown of its slaty-grey head and cheeks, and its bill is black.

Rock-hopper Penguin

The muddy yellow waters of the Plata extend outwards to the sea and here the observer will be more interested to watch the approaching shipping passing to port in the long buoyed channel with Montevideo to starboard and the busy docks and waterfront of Buenos Aires looming up ahead.

ROUTE 9

British Isles to Port Said and
Aden – The Gulf of Aden

As a ship clears harbour and shapes course down the English Channel, a flock of **Lesser Black-backed Gulls (27, 34, 40)** and **Herring Gulls (28, 35, 40)** will almost certainly be following astern, planing without effort in the up-draught above the ship and swooping to settle in the wake at intervals, as opportunity is being taken to dump refuse from the galley. As they swoop towards the pickings the difference between the upperwing plumage of the two species in adult plumage will be evident, although it may not be easy to differentiate between the mottled juveniles.

A few **Northern Black-headed Gulls (28, 31, 32, 37, 40)**, and in winter months even a **Common Gull (28, 35, 40)** or two, may be in company at the outset, but in mid-Channel these two most inshore of gulls rarely follow ships.

As the ship proceeds westwards a lookout should be kept for the more offshore seabirds, although never in quantity. The most conspicuous, possibly only the sighting of a single or pair of birds, is without doubt the **Northern Gannet (18)**. The largest of the N. Atlantic seabirds, this cigar-shaped majestic white bird, in adult plumage with its long narrow black tipped wings, stands out conspicuously in flight. The nearest breeding colony is in the Channel Is., though this species also breeds in Brittany, and it will be when passing to the north of these islands that the most likely opportunity of sighting gannets may occur.

Three species of the auk family, the **Common Guillemot (46)**, the **Razorbill (46)** and the **Atlantic Puffin (47)**, offshore feeders capturing the smaller fish by pursuing them underwater, occur in the English Channel and are frequently to be seen

Common Cormorant

outside their breeding season when they remain at sea. They are more likely to be seen in the western half of the Channel, either in small flocks or 'rafts' on the water or, when disturbed, flying low over the sea with direct whirring flight. All three species appear almost black above with mainly white underparts; small stubby birds easily recognised as a family but often difficult to identify at sea at any distance.

The **Common Cormorant (20)**, which normally feeds close offshore, becomes more widespread along the south coast of England in the autumn and winter and may occasionally be seen in mid-Channel: a large black-looking seabird with long sinuous neck flying with steady wing-beats low over the sea.

Cormorants also have the habit of perching on posts and marker buoys with wings spread to dry. The **Shag (21)** prefers rocks and cliffs, is more restricted to the west coast of England and is rarely seen at sea.

The western approaches

On reaching the more open waters of the western approaches the first oceanic seabirds are likely to be seen – the **British Storm-petrel (13)**, the **Manx Shearwater (9)**, the **Common Kittiwake (33, 39)** and the **Northern Fulmar (11)**. The British Storm-petrel, Manx Shearwater and Common Kittiwake all breed on the west coasts and islands of the British Isles, the little storm-petrel nesting in crevices in cliffs and stone walls, the Manx Shearwater in underground burrows in the soft springy turf which crowns the hinterland of cliff edges, the Common Kittiwake on the smallest handholds and ledges of the steepest cliffs. The Northern Fulmar has been steadily extending its breeding range southwards in recent years from its original stronghold on the wider ledges of the tall stacks of St Kilda.

The Manx Shearwater is more likely to be seen between spring and late summer, for in the autumn it disperses southwards from its breeding quarters into the open ocean, some wintering as far away as the east coast of S. America. Unlike the gulls, it is less easily spotted, for one's eyes must range widely over the grey surface of the sea for a glimpse of this oceanic bird planing low over the swell, showing at one moment the black of its upperparts and at the next the white of its underparts as it tilts and shearwaters on rigid wings.

The British Storm-petrel is one of three very similar tiny dark storm-petrels likely to be seen as the voyage proceeds, the British Storm-petrel, Wilson's Storm-petrel and Leach's Storm-petrel. Known to seafarers as 'Mother Cary's Chickens', storm-petrels are the smallest seabirds. They are easily recognised as a family but prove difficult to identify individually at sea without the closest observation of minor differences in plumage and flight characteristics.

The first sighting of this little sooty-black bird, showing a white patch of feathers above the rump with a square, not forked, tail, may well be as it flutters to and fro across the white wake of the ship, sometimes dropping its legs into the churned-up foam, for British Storm-petrels, although not regular ship followers, are often seen astern.

Lesser Black-backed and Herring Gulls may occasionally pick up and follow ships at this early stage in the passage but with Ushant Lighthouse still in sight to port, Common Kittiwakes and an occasional Northern Fulmar are now likely to be seen. Adult Common Kittiwakes, although at a casual glance somewhat similar to the Common Gull, are more lightly built, flying with a swifter, graceful, buoyant flight often close over the sea, and a sight of completely black wing tips should be the first point to look for. Young birds in immature plumage are, however, conspicuously different. During June and July Common Kittiwakes forsake the open oceans to a great extent, relying on obtaining food for their nestlings at a lesser distance from their breeding cliffs. At other seasons they are entirely oceanic and may be seen in considerable numbers throughout the Bay of Biscay.

Northern Fulmars are now seen regularly in the western approaches. Being of an inquisitive nature they have a habit of closing ships, often giving a splendid opportunity of studying their aerodynamic appearance and magnificent planing flight as they glide close by on stiffly held wings.

The Bay of Biscay

During the crossing of the Bay of Biscay a ship will pass beyond the normal range of inshore and offshore seabirds. **Great Black-backed Gulls (27, 34, 40)**, Lesser Black-backed Gulls and Northern Gannets are occasionally seen, more frequently in the autumn and winter as numbers move southwards.

Common Kittiwakes will continue to be seen throughout the crossing; more rarely will a Northern Fulmar be seen, and the latter is more likely to disappear before a ship sights the Spanish coast.

The sighting of a **Great Skua (26)** is a regular feature in the Bay of Biscay. This rather large heavily built brown seabird showing pale wing patches often picks up ships, following astern for a period. If any scraps are thrown overboard you may be sure that it will be seen away astern gobbling up the titbits.

At the appropriate seasons a lookout should be kept over the sea's surface for two new shearwaters, the **Cory's** and **Great Shearwaters (9)**, both considerably larger and browner above and more heavily built than the Manx Shearwater which may have been seen earlier. In a fresh wind they may be seen gliding over the crests of the swell, or in calm windless weather assisting their normal shearwatering by a series of steady wing-beats. At first appearance both species look very similar and a careful study of their detailed descriptions is needed to determine the particular points of difference.

Cory's Shearwaters breed on the eastern Atlantic islands and on the Berlengas off Portugal, and may be seen in the Bay of Biscay at all seasons, though in greater numbers during the summer and early autumn. Numbers disperse southwards to winter off the west coasts of S. Africa.

The Great Shearwater is but a seasonal migrant to the N. Atlantic between April and November, and does not arrive in the vicinity of the Bay of Biscay until September, increasing in numbers during October. Some late arrivals may be seen in November, possibly immature non-breeding birds without the same call to hasten southwards.

A third shearwater, the **Sooty Shearwater (8)**, like the Great Shearwater also a migrant from the far S. Atlantic winter and following a generally similar route, may possibly be seen in the Bay during the autumn. It appears to spread into the N. Atlantic in smaller numbers and is seen much less frequently in the area, usually singly or in pairs. However, its smaller build, much darker appearance – its looks almost black at sea except for its pale central underwing-coverts – and quicker wing-beats between short glides, will invite attention.

The British Storm-petrel has been more likely to appear at the outset, but in the southern quarter of the Bay **Wilson's** and **Leach's Storm-petrels (13)** predominate in their due seasons. Here again one cannot stress too strongly the difficulty of differentiating between the species without the closest scrutiny of plumage and other characteristics.

Wilson's Storm-petrel, however, is also a migrant visitor to the N. Atlantic. Very large numbers cross the Equator northwards in March and April, and although a few may be seen along the route as early as May they are most likely to be seen during their southward movement from early October onwards. Shipping records certainly indicate their appearance at this season, following in the wake of ships.

Leach's Storm-petrels breed in the N. Atlantic on the outer islands off the N.W. coast of Scotland and off the east coasts of N. America and Canada, but they spread widely across the Atlantic too and may be seen in most months of the year. They are somewhat larger and browner in appearance than Wilson's, with a stronger bounding erratic flight, paying little attention to ships.

The two smaller skuas, the **Arctic** and **Pomarine Skuas (25)**, have been identified occasionally along the route during the periods of their migrations in April/May and more often in September/October, but their principal migration route takes them further to the west, and they are rarely seen.

They are smaller, have narrower more pointed wings and a swifter more hawk-like flight than the Great Skua, and occur in both a light and dark phase in plumage. The Pomarine Skua is more addicted to following ships for a short period.

As a ship rounds Cape Finisterre a few of the gulls of the types seen at the start of the voyage may once again appear.

Cape Finisterre to Gibraltar

Southward from Finisterre the route begins to pass close to the coasts of Spain and Portugal.

Northern Gannets, Common Kittiwakes and an occasional Great Skua are likely to be seen, and gulls tend to gather around fishing vessels off the coast. The Berlengas Is. off Portugal are the breeding ground of many seabirds including Cory's Shearwaters, and while these may be seen at all seasons, the Great Shearwater does not appear to range regularly so far to the eastward in the autumn. The Great Black-backed Gull, Lesser Black-backed Gull and Herring Gull have all been observed along the route, increasing in numbers during the late autumn and winter.

Approaching the Straits of Gibraltar

The sea area to the west of the Straits, and indeed in the narrow waters of the Straits, is a focal area for a variety of seabirds, particularly in the winter and early spring. Manx Shearwaters have been seen regularly in September where it seems probable that they loiter during their southward migration; Northern Gannets, the majority in their speckled brown immature plumage, have often been observed, sometimes in considerable numbers in the late autumn, to the west of the Straits, where flocks of Cory's Shearwaters and both British and Wilson's Storm-petrels also occur. Rarely Common Guillemots, Razorbills and Atlantic Puffins have been reported. From August onwards, records also show sightings of **Grey Phalaropes (25)** on southward migration.

On entering the Straits the observer may have the alternative attraction of sighting schools of porpoises breaking surface around the ship, and the dorsal fins of larger Black Fish moving more sedately through the water. With the view of the distant shore of N. Africa to starboard and the white tower of Tarifa Lighthouse ahead to port, Lesser Black-backed Gulls and Common Gulls, frequently in winter months, follow lazily behind the ship. However, a sharp eye may pick out a Herring Gull not quite like the usual run. Its legs may be seen to be yellow, its mantle and upperwings of a somewhat darker shade, and yet not as dark as a Lesser Black-backed Gull. For here, and indeed onwards, the yellow-legged form of the **Herring Gull (28, 35, 40)** may be seen mingling with the flesh-coloured-legged Herring Gulls.

As the Rock of Gibraltar is now in sight and the great lump of the Apes Hill looms up above the N. African shore, a flock of Cory's Shearwaters is a frequent sight beyond Gibraltar Bay.

The western Mediterranean

Voyagers in ships on the direct main route to Port Said are likely to be disappointed by the scarcity of seabirds, for these are mainly inshore species which do not wander far from the many harbours along the coasts. It is in ships trading coastwise that more opportunities arise.

Leaving Gibraltar, some of the gulls already mentioned may follow the ship to sea. In April and May, and again in September and October, numbers of migrating **Black Terns (44)** cross the Mediterranean in the vicinity of the eastern end of the Straits. During these seasons one may be fortunate enough to sight one of these strikingly-plumaged dark terns. Its entirely black body and head and lead-grey upperparts of the spring and summer months will have reverted to a mottled head and white underparts by the autumn.

Wilson's Storm-petrels and British Storm-petrels both penetrate into the western Mediterranean, the latter breeding on some Mediterranean islands. Northern Gannets also penetrate into the Mediterranean in winter months. At this stage a lookout should be kept for the **Balearic Shearwater (9)**, a race of the Manx Shearwater, similar in size and flight, but with a palish brown underbody.

Offshore along the coast of N. Africa the yellow-legged form of the Herring Gull may be seen amongst the flesh-coloured-legged Herring Gulls. On this coastal route three coast-loving gulls have been observed. The **Little Gull (31, 32, 37)** is but a winter visitor and is most likely to be seen in winter or immature plumage. Its particularly small size, pale wings and, in adults, its lead-grey underwings should immediately attract attention. The **Slender-billed Gull (29, 37)** may be seen at all seasons, though it tends to hug the coastline. It is somewhat larger and similar to the Northern Black-headed Gull but its head is always white. **Audouin's Gull (29, 35)** winters in flocks along this northern coast of Africa but clings close to the shoreline. In adult plumage somewhat similar in size to the Herring Gull, its red bill, showing a black cross band, and black legs help to distinguish it.

The central Mediterranean

Passing through the Malta Channel one may again notice Cory's Shearwaters. They are recorded as breeding on the Maltese islands, where the British Storm-petrel has also been known to breed.

In the winter months another species of gull commonly seen in Malta harbour is sometimes seen on the sea route. This is the **Mediterranean Black-headed Gull (32, 37)**. Look for its entirely white primary wing feathers, and in winter the absence of its dark hood.

The eastern Mediterranean

There is usually a marked absence of seabirds along this part of the route until close off Port Said. A few yellow-legged Herring Gulls, a Lesser Black-backed Gull or two in winter and spring and Cory's Shearwaters. Very occasionally the **Levantine Shearwater (9)**, the Aegean race of the Manx Shearwater, has been seen.

Port Said

The beaches, dunes and mudflats which divide Lake Manzala from the sea near Port Said provide a focal point at the eastern end of the Mediterranean for numbers of resident and migratory gulls and terns.

In Port Said harbour one may see yellow-legged Herring Gulls, Mediterranean Black-headed Gulls, Lesser Black-backed Gulls and Northern Black-headed Gulls, the last two species in great numbers in winter and early spring. Little Gulls, Slender-billed Gulls and the **Red Sea Black-headed Gull**, now often known as the **White-eyed Gull (32, 37, 40)**, have been recorded in small numbers. The Great Black-backed Gull and even on one occasion a Northern Gannet have been observed off the harbour in winter, but the gannet is certainly exceptional.

The Red Sea Black-headed Gull differs markedly from other black-headed gulls to be seen in the area by its darker slate-grey plumage, its white eyelids and deep black hood in breeding plumage.

Among the terns, the **Caspian Tern (41)** and Little Tern are those more likely to be seen off the shoreline at the harbour entrance. The Caspian Tern is conspicuous amongst terns on account of its outstandingly large size, and at close quarters by its large stout red bill.

The Suez Canal

With the great expanse of Lake Manzala close at hand any of the seabirds listed under Port Said may be seen at the outset. Alas, with the closure of the Suez Canal and military operations, the sight of the flocks of flamingoes among the other waders and wildfowl which used to be seen feeding on the wetlands beside the Canal at the beginning of the transit may be past history. Later, save for the passage through Lake Timsah and the Bitter Lakes, the Canal is bordered by the most arid desert as far as the eye can see.

Suez anchorage

Ships lying at anchor attract the presence of gulls. Of these the Red Sea Black-headed Gull is the commonest at all seasons and yellow-legged Herring and Mediterranean Black-headed Gulls are frequently present. During winter months Lesser Black-backed and Northern Black-headed Gulls are sometimes plentiful. Slender-billed Gulls, Caspian and Little Terns have also been reported.

Gulf of Suez and Red Sea

At the outset the Red Sea Black-headed Gull is the commonest, but seabirds are not plentiful. Here, too, if the voyager is fortunate enough to be passing through the Gulf of Suez during the first week of April or the last ten days of August, he may be a witness to the mass migration of White Storks passing in thousands across the Gulf during their northerly and southerly seasonal migrations.

As the ship enters the Red Sea the yellow shores and barren hills of the Sinai Peninsula will soon be left behind. Although the ship will be proceeding through relatively narrow waters seabirds in the central portion are usually scarce until the southern end of the route is approached. The weather in the Red Sea can at times be unbearable. The hot air from the arid mountains of Saudi Arabia and the Yemen brings with it an atmosphere laden with fine particles of sand, the consequent heat haze shutting seabirds from sight. On rare occasions, the Red Sea has appeared as if covered with patches of floating red sand which is nothing else but countless millions of Noctiluca, a small jelly the size of a pin's head with an orange-red centre. Hundreds of tons may be washed ashore covering the beaches with what appears to be blood. Doubtless this is the origin of the sea's name. But to continue. From December onwards Lesser Black-backed Gulls are moving northwards and may pick up the ship for a while.

South of approximately 17°N. a variety of new species may be expected. In summer months in particular considerable numbers of **Brown-winged** or **Bridled Terns (44)**, **Crested** and **Lesser-crested Terns (41)** are likely to be seen. **White-cheeked Terns (42)** and Little Terns occur in small numbers, and the first **Aden Gull (32, 37, 40)** will appear. The white forehead patch, the palish-brown upperparts, contrasting with the white underparts, will call attention to the

Aden Gull

Brown-winged Tern, but this species is easily confused with the rather similar Sooty Tern. Here again the Aden Gull is easily mistaken for a Red Sea Black-headed Gull. At this stage it is helpful to study the detailed descriptions of these species in advance.

Towards the southern end of the Red Sea the route passes close to a number of small desolate rocky islands which comprise the Zubair, Abu Ail and Hanish groups. The Red Sea Black-headed and Aden Gulls may still be seen. **Brown Boobies (19)** nest on these islands in considerable numbers together with a few

Blue-faced Boobies (18). The voyager is certain to see these large seabirds, which belong to the same family as the Northern Gannet and have the same characteristic flight, plunging headlong into the sea when fishing.

Here too the graceful **Red-billed Tropic-bird (15)** may be seen for the first time. These beautiful white birds, with their long streaming marline spike tail feathers and quick strong wing-beats, usually seen flying high overhead, are quite unmistakable as a family but each species has certain different plumage characteristics.

There is little evidence of the oceanic shearwaters and petrels penetrating any great distance within the confined waters of the Red Sea. In winter months however **Persian Shearwaters (10)** are usually present, sometimes in considerable flocks, and from June until October Wilson's Storm-petrels range into the Red Sea from the Gulf of Aden.

The Persian Shearwater is the only shearwater likely to be seen within the Red Sea, medium-small and stocky, dark brown above with whitish central underparts.

Passing the Bab el Mandeb and the barren outline of Perim I. with the distant mountains of the Yemen to port, it is but a short haul to Aden.

The Gulf of Aden

The Gulf of Aden is a focal point for many seabirds at different seasons, the largest concentrations occurring relatively close to the coast of S.E. Arabia during the period of the south-west monsoon between May and October. In the coastal waters at this season the sea is driven offshore, causing an upwelling turbulence which brings nutrient salts to the surface, producing plankton and rich marine feed in the surface layers. Ships passing to and from the Persian Gulf have noted frequently a yellowish surface scum and 'fishy' odour on passage during these sea conditions. Marked phosphorescence is seen at night.

Seasonal distribution of seabirds

The occurrence of different species in the Gulf of Aden is related to the seasonal distribution of certain seabirds which occur north of the Equator in the Indian Ocean. In general, those which breed on the Indian Ocean islands north of the Equator may be seen at all seasons of the year, bearing in mind that only truly oceanic species such as the shearwaters, petrels, storm-petrels, Sooty Terns and tropic-birds range far out into the ocean, much of which in the tropical zone of warm surface water provides very little surface feed.

There are, however, a few shearwaters, petrels and storm-petrels whose breeding quarters are confined to areas far south of the Equator and which migrate into the northern Indian Ocean and Arabian Sea in the early part of the southern winter.

In the Gulf of Aden three 'tubenose' species, which may be labelled loosely as 'resident', are most likely to be seen for they are present at all seasons – Persian Shearwater, a local race of Audubon's Shearwater, the **Wedge-tailed Shearwater (7)** and **Jouanin's Petrel (7)**, the latter two liable to be mistaken for one another.

The most difficult task facing an observer at all times at sea lies in identifying correctly the different species of shearwaters, petrels and storm-petrels. Finer points in plumage pattern, often requiring great discernment, shapes of bills and tails, and special characteristics in flight must be looked for.

Look for the white in the central portion of underwings and underparts and the short round tail in the Persian Shearwater, the long slender grey bill and long wedge-shaped tail in the all-dark Wedge-tailed Shearwater (for it is only found in its dark phase in the Gulf of Aden), the short thick black bill, flesh-coloured legs and the swooping flight of the uniformly brownish-black Jouanin's Petrel.

STORM-PETRELS AND PHALAROPES. The Gulf of Aden is notable for the large flocks of Wilson's Storm-petrels which spend the northern summer and autumn months on the western side of the N. Indian Ocean and Arabian Sea. They probably cross the Equator from the south in April and are returning by the end of October. Large numbers are often seen following in the wake of ships from July onwards, and are the only storm-petrels likely to be seen.

During the autumn and winter months large flocks of **Red-necked Phalaropes (25)** appear in the Gulf. These small dainty waders migrate southwards from their breeding areas on land in high northern latitudes, to winter at sea where surface feed is abundant along the offshore waters from the Gulf of Oman to the Gulf of Aden. They are most frequent between October and February in their winter plumage. Some may still be present in March before returning northwards, but it is doubtful whether these will have donned their smart summer plumage.

Red-necked Phalaropes in this area have sometimes been mistaken for White-faced Storm-petrels; the latter however never occur in flocks, nor do they settle on the water, as phalaropes do frequently, and they have entirely different flight characteristics. Moreover the White-faced Storm-petrels are to be seen further out at sea and only in the summer months, and unlikely to occur in the Gulf of Aden even then.

Other seabirds

Aden Gulls pick up and follow ships from time to time in the Gulf of Aden; Brown-winged, Crested and Lesser-crested Terns are always likely to be seen; the Red-billed Tropic-bird is often reported (neither the White-tailed nor Red-tailed species occur), and an occasional Brown Booby may be seen. The Blue-faced Booby is much less common in the area.

Aden to the Persian Gulf

The sea passage from Aden to the Persian Gulf provides an unusually interesting variety of seabirds throughout the whole length of the route, a great influx occurring close off the coasts of the Yemen Republic, Muscat and Oman during the peak of the south-west monsoon in July. Large numbers of shearwaters, petrels, Wilson's Storm-petrels and terns may occur. During the period of the quiet north-east monsoon between late autumn and early spring the surface feed offshore diminishes and seabirds tend to drift away north-eastwards, whilst an invasion of Red-necked Phalaropes arrives from high northern latitudes to winter at sea in this favourite area.

Leaving Aden

The route to Ras ai Hadd passes relatively close to headlands and islands and within range of most inshore and offshore seabirds. **Aden Gulls (32, 37, 40)** are seen regularly at all seasons, more particularly during the southern half of the passage, and **Lesser Black-backed Gulls (27, 34, 40)** at some points along the whole route from autumn to early spring. **Northern Black-headed Gulls (28, 31, 32, 37, 40)** cling close

Lesser-crested Tern

inshore and occur more frequently in harbours in the Persian Gulf in winter months. **Brown-winged** or **Bridled Terns (44)**, **Crested** and **Lesser-crested Terns (41)** are always likely to be seen in the Gulf of Aden at all seasons, and on occasion **Brown Booby (19)**, **Blue-faced Booby (18)** and **Red-billed Tropic-bird (15)**.

Northwards to the Straits of Hormuz

During the route northwards not only are certain species of shearwaters and petrels to be seen at all seasons, but an influx of migrant shearwaters, storm-petrels, skuas, and phalaropes appear during certain months, while gulls, terns, boobies and tropic-birds may add to the list.

At all seasons **Wedge-tailed Shearwaters (7)**, **Jouanin's Petrels (9)** and **Persian Shearwaters (10)**, a race of Audubon's Shearwater, are almost certain to be seen. The first named is distinctive with its overall dark brown plumage, long slender grey bill and outstandingly long wedge-shaped tail. Jouanin's Petrel is smaller, also brownish-black with a short thick black bill and much swifter swooping flight. The Persian Shearwater is the only one which will show any white on its underparts and underwings. Persian Shearwaters are often seen in flocks in the Straits of Hormuz and within the Persian Gulf.

MIGRANT SHEARWATERS AND STORM-PETRELS. Another large, uniformly chocolate brown shearwater, the **Pale-footed Shearwater (8)**, appears along the route in late summer from July to late September, but does not penetrate within the Persian Gulf. It breeds on islands off S.W. Australia during the southern summer, and undertakes a circuit of the N. Indian Ocean and Arabian Sea during the southern winter, appearing to start its return journey somewhat east of the shipping route towards the end of September. More heavily-built than the Wedge-tailed Shearwater, its chief distinction is in its long straw-coloured bill, short round tail and more laboured flight.

The most notable influx from June onwards to October is that of the **Wilson's Storm-petrel (13)**. Huge flocks collect along the route during the period of the south-west monsoon. Apart from Wilson's Storm-petrel, the only other migrant storm-petrel from south of the Equator which may possibly be seen is the **White-faced Storm-petrel (13)** which spreads into the Arabian Sea in small numbers during the summer months. It appears to keep well out to seaward outside the normal shipping route, but nevertheless has been recorded on some passages between May and September. Its appearance will attract attention at once, the white face, dusky eye patch, greyish upperparts and white underparts. It is usually seen singly and must not be confused with phalaropes in winter plumage, for indeed it will have left the Arabian Sea on its return journey south before the main autumn and winter invasion of the phalaropes occurs.

PHALAROPES. The area of upwelling in the Arabian Sea is one of several localities around the globe at which similar conditions prevail, providing suitable food and wintering quarters at sea for phalaropes.

Large flocks of these small dainty waders are seen regularly from autumn onwards all the way from the Gulf of Aden to the Gulf of Oman for this is the resort of the **Red-necked Phalarope (25)**. It seems doubtful if **Grey Phalaropes (25)** occur in any numbers if at all.

North of 15°N.

The Blue-faced Booby largely replaces the Brown Booby, and large numbers of the former may be seen off the barren Kuria Muria Is. where a breeding colony exists. Beyond Ras al Hadd numbers diminish and they do not appear to occur regularly within the Persian Gulf. The Red-billed Tropic-bird has been seen frequently as far north as the Straits of Hormuz however.

During the period of spring and autumn migrations, March/April and September/October, **Pomarine Skuas (26)** are seen occasionally and **Great Skuas (26)** on rare occasions.

Ras al Hadd to within the Persian Gulf

From Ras al Hadd to the Straits of Hormuz, Wedge-tailed Shearwaters and Persian Shearwaters are a common sight, the Persian Shearwaters sometimes in large flocks. Wilson's Storm-petrels and Red-necked Phalaropes also congregate here in large numbers at the appropriate seasons.

Sooty Terns (44) and **White-cheeked Terns (42)** are known to breed in large numbers on Daimaniyat Is. (23°35′N., 57°59′E.) during July and a lookout should be kept for sightings at this season.

Once within the Gulf, the Persian Shearwater holds sway and Wedge-tailed Shearwaters become much scarcer. Red-billed Tropic-birds are likely to be seen in the Gulf of Oman and Straits of Hormuz. They have been reported as breeding on

Persian form of Audubon's Shearwater

Jazirat Tawakul I., a small rocky island close to the main shipping route inside the Quoin Is., on Nabi-u-Tanb and Umn al Moradim, with eggs in late April. This is the only species of the tropic-bird family in the area.

The **Socotra Cormorant (20)** is the common resident species, easily recognised by its entirely glossy-black plumage and soft parts. It breeds on islands between January and March. Enormous flocks have been seen after the breeding season ends, apparently migrating between the islands. The continental race of the **Common Cormorant (20)** is seen occasionally but its status is uncertain.

GULLS AND TERNS. The chief feature is the variety of gulls and terns that are either resident or seasonal. In the winter months large numbers of **Northern**

Black-headed Gulls, **Lesser Black-backed** and **Herring Gulls (28, 35, 40)** are present and some Common Gulls. Considerable numbers of **Slender-billed Gulls (29, 37)** also occur. At all seasons Aden Gulls may be seen, chiefly in the eastern approaches to the Gulf and occasionally **Great Black-headed Gulls (32, 37)** are seen. Terns however provide the greatest variety and numbers. **Brown-winged** or **Bridled Terns (44)**, White-cheeked Terns, **Caspian Terns (41)** and **Little Terns (43)** occur in the greatest numbers, together with **Crested** and **Lesser-crested Terns (41)**. **Sandwich Terns (41, 43)**, **Gull-billed Terns (43)** and, more rarely, **White-winged Black Terns (44)** have been seen.

While it is not possible to quote all possible breeding areas, it is known that Brown-winged Terns, White-cheeked Terns and Lesser-crested Terns breed on Al Jurayd I. (27°11′N., 49°52′E.) during June, Brown-winged, White-cheeked and Caspian Terns on Khubbar I., and White-cheeked and Little Terns on Bahrain with eggs and young in June.

Finally, if a pelican is seen, no doubt it will be the **Dalmatian Pelican (16)**.

Aden to New Zealand

The seabirds of the Gulf of Aden have been described in Route 9. Thereafter the sea route entails a long haul across the entire breadth of the tropical belt of the Indian Ocean when days may pass without a seabird being sighted.

As the ship leaves the Gulf to pass Cape Guardafui and Socotra I. **Brown Boobies (19)**, **Blue-faced Boobies (18)**, **Red-billed Tropic-birds (15)**, **Aden Gulls (32, 37, 40)** and possibly **Common Noddies (44)** may be seen. Although the **Socotra Cormorant (20)** breeds on Socotra it clings to the coast and is not likely to be seen.

The mid-ocean passage

The route quickly outranges all but the most oceanic species, but **Sooty Terns (44)** which nest in large colonies, together with many other seabirds, on the island groups in the Seychelles wander far out into the ocean. **Jouanin's Petrel (9)** may be seen off Socotra but the **Wedge-tailed Shearwater (7)** is undoubtedly the more likely

Wedge-tailed Shearwater

of these two species to be seen as the voyage proceeds. The most noticeable points of difference between the two are referred to at the conclusion of Route 9.

Certain storm-petrels and at least one shearwater, which breed on islands in the southern Indian Ocean and sub-antarctic regions, migrate northwards during the southern winter and appear in the Indian Ocean north of the Equator in May and June, reaching the Arabian Sea and returning south of the Equator during October. Of these **Wilson's Storm-petrel (13)** is the most numerous. While these migrants have been plotted in some cases with regular frequency on reaching their northerly limits, and a guide to some probable lanes of migration indicated, none can tell as yet the extent of their distribution across the central portion of the Indian Ocean. Apart from the probability of sighting Wilson's Storm-petrel, there is considerably less chance in the mid-ocean of seeing the following:

Pale-footed Shearwater (8). Breeds on islands off S.W. Australia and appears to migrate northwards in the eastern quarter of the Indian Ocean, probably crossing the Equator about May and circling in an anti-clockwise direction into the Arabian Sea. It can be distinguished from the Wedge-tailed Shearwater by its long straw-coloured bill, short round tail and more laboured flight.

The **White-faced Storm-petrel (13)** also reaches the Arabian Sea. Its white face, dusky eye patch, greyish-brown upperparts and white underparts are noticeable.

White-bellied and **Black-bellied Storm-petrels (13)**, if seen at all!, for their appearance in mid-ocean is rare, are most likely to be seen hopping and fluttering in the ship's wake. Identification is difficult for the white area of the underbody varies.

Swinhoe's Storm-petrel (14). This all dark storm-petrel, with a slightly forked tail, which breeds in islands off Formosa (Taiwan) and disperses towards the East Indies, is now known to extend across the northern Indian Ocean. Only a few specimens have been observed.

Passing the Chagos Archipelago

The islands are the haunt and breeding areas of many tropical seabirds, but the sea route will pass outside the range of the more inshore species – so Black-naped Terns, the delicate White Terns, and the Common and Lesser Noddies are unlikely to be seen. The Sooty Terns, **White-tailed** and **Red-tailed Tropic-birds (15)** range far out to sea however, and for the first time in all likelihood frigate-birds may be seen. Black with long narrow wings and deeply forked tails, these sinister birds are often seen circling high overhead waiting to harry other seabirds. Identification of particular species needs careful observation. In the Chagos Is. the **Lesser Frigate-bird (24)** is the resident species. There will be little difficulty in spotting the difference between the adults of the two tropic-birds if the colour of their long marline spike central tail feathers is noted; immatures of both species are almost identical however.

South of the Tropic of Capricorn

Between latitude 15°S. and the Tropic of Capricorn very little seabird life is normally encountered. For the first time the **Soft-plumaged Petrel (10)** may be seen flying low over the sea. It is not unlike the White-faced Storm-petrel at first sight, but considerably larger and one should look for the dark underwing and dark chest band.

Towards Australia

From now onwards an increasing variety of seabirds will appear daily. The Wedge-tailed and Pale-footed Shearwater, White-faced and Wilson's Storm-petrels may be seen. The Soft-plumaged Petrel will increase in numbers and a whole range of seabirds of the southern oceans will begin to put in an appearance. Many of these tend to disperse somewhat further north into temperate latitudes during the southern winter (July, August, September). In the region of 25°S. albatrosses are likely to pick up the ship and follow, and in all probability the very first to be seen will be the great **Wandering Albatross (3)**. Those which we see furthest north during the southern winter are sure to include many in varying stages of immature plumage. It will be wise to study the detailed descriptions of the albatrosses in advance, for well before rounding Cape Leeuwin **Yellow-nosed** and **Black-browed Albatrosses (5)** will also be seen almost daily, picking up the ship at dawn and increasing in numbers throughout the day.

One other albatross, usually not encountered until south of Australia, but unmistakable on account of its overall sooty-brown plumage, will be the **Sooty Albatross (6)**. This is seen quite regularly throughout the Great Australian Bight. Seen rarely, as its normal range appears to be generally further south, is the somewhat similar **Light-mantled Sooty Albatross (6)**.

Across the Great Australian Bight

The southern ocean south of the great land masses of S. America, S. Africa and Australia is the happy hunting ground of such a variety of oceanic seabirds of the order Procellariiformes that no-one can tell with certainty in what sequence these will be seen from a ship passing across the Great Australian Bight. Yet some early sightings can be postulated. The **Little Shearwater (9)** breeds on islands off S.W. Australia and does not appear to range far afield, for reports from ships are confined to this area on the route. The **Grey-faced Petrel (10)** also breeds on the south coast of Western Australia and is reported regularly in the area at all seasons.

Some species are certainly seen more frequently than others. The Wandering, Black-browed and Yellow-nosed Albatrosses once they have picked up a ship never let it go, though some birds may replace others. Of the petrels, the **Pintado Petrel (11)** is the greatest ship follower of all, picking up ships even north of the Tropic of Capricorn, at times often flying in flocks, and of such a distinctive piebald plumage that it is unmistakable. When crossing the Bight too the **Giant Petrel** (Nelly or Stinker) **(6, 7)** is to be seen almost daily, and one would be unlucky if one did not see the **White-chinned Petrel** (Shoemaker or Cape Hen) **(7)**. This large dark petrel with a distinctive white chin and massive pale bill assiduously follows ships. In addition, flocks of the small **prions (11)** are seen frequently. These little birds with their grey-blue upperparts, dark W pattern, white underparts and grey wedge-shaped tail with a black band, tilt and turn low over the sea in flight, and it is impossible to distinguish between the various species at sea. In this area they will probably be Fairy Prions. In winter months White-headed Petrels also occur in the Bight.

Apart from the 'tubenoses', the southern **Great Skua (26)** is one of the most regular seabirds to be seen across the whole length of the Great Australian Bight at all seasons, and it picks up and follows ships, waiting to pounce on garbage or chase and harry other seabirds in the vicinity. It is indistinguishable from the Great Skua of the northern seas. Several instances have occurred of these skuas settling in the rigging.

Rounding the southern tip of Western Australia the ship may come within range of a few of the more inshore and offshore seabirds which occupy these coasts. Of these the **Australian Gannet (18)** is quite common and is more likely to be seen than the **Pacific Gull (27, 34, 40)** and the smaller more delicate **Silver Gull (29, 38, 40)**, all of which are resident in Australia.

The Bass Strait and Tasman Sea

All the seabirds already described during the crossing of the Great Australian Bight are equally likely to be seen in the Bass Strait and during the crossing of the Tasman Sea. The many islands and relatively narrow waters of the Bass Strait provide opportunities for some of the less oceanic seabirds to appear. The Australian Gannet, Pacific and Silver Gulls, the Crested Tern, **Little** and **Fairy Terns (43)** may be seen though infrequently, but the cormorants, of which there are several different species common to the southern Australian coasts, have not figured in any reports from ships, no doubt remaining too close inshore to be seen on the main shipping route.

The islands and mainland of Tasmania form the principal breeding stations of the **Short-tailed Shearwater (8)**. Known locally as the 'Mutton Bird', it leaves these breeding quarters in April/May after the young have fledged and undertakes a vast clockwise migratory sweep northwards into high latitudes in the N. Pacific Ocean returning again about October to occupy its nesting areas. From May to October few if any will be seen, but between November and April the Short-tailed Shearwaters often present an amazing spectacle. The sea may be churned white with thousands of these birds plunging with threshing wings into the sea's surface, as fish leap on all sides.

Before leaving Australian waters some mention should be made of those great globe-spanning migrants – the **Arctic** and **Pomarine Skuas (26)**. Breeding in high latitudes in the northern hemisphere they leave on their great southward migration in September on a wide front, and some winter regularly in the sea areas south of Australia and off New Zealand. In February ships on the route have reported small parties of these skuas, on one occasion in March up to 200, on a date when they might well be congregating prior to commencing their northward migration.

The Tasman Sea to Wellington, New Zealand

Wandering, Black-browed, Yellow-nosed, Shy and Sooty Albatrosses; Wedge-tailed, Pale-footed and Little Shearwaters; Giant, Grey-faced, White-chinned and Pintado Petrels; Wilson's and White-faced Storm-petrels, and the southern Great Skua are all to be seen in the Tasman Sea.

To add to this selection further species common to the S. Pacific Ocean and New Zealand waters may be seen for the first time. Three new albatrosses, the **Grey-headed Albatross (5)**, **Buller's Albatross (4)** and the very large **Royal Albatross (3)** have been recorded, but are perhaps more likely to be seen in the eastern quarter of the Tasman Sea. There are many shearwaters and petrels amongst this proliferation of seabirds, but not all will be referred to in detail. The 'Cookilaria' and 'Hypoleuca' groups of petrels are in most cases so similar in appearance that even expert observers find difficulty in identifying the separate species at sea. Of the new shearwaters and petrels the *****Sooty Shearwater (8)**, the 'Mutton Bird' of New Zealand, **Fluttering Shearwater (10)**, and *****Grey-backed Shearwater(8)** are the most likely to be identified, together with the **White-headed Petrel (11)**, the *****Peale's Petrel (12)** and the **Parkinson's Petrel (7)**.

The White-bellied Storm-petrel which may have been seen earlier on the route,

* These species are likely to be absent between May and October during their distant northward migrations.

the Black-bellied Storm-petrel, and both occur in the Tasman Sea, and here also the **Common Diving-petrel (14)** and the small **prions (11)**, all of which may have been observed earlier in the Bass Strait.

Wellington Harbour

A passenger in a ship approaching and entering harbour is unlikely to have the opportunity of observing many seabirds which from time to time visit the environs of the harbour approaches. Only those more likely to be seen are mentioned.

The Wandering Albatross and Giant Petrel visit the harbour sometimes, sitting on the water close alongside ships. Australian Gannets may be seen diving for fish, and four species of cormorants, the **Common Cormorant (20, 23)**, **Pied**, **Little Pied** and rarely the **Spotted Cormorants (22)** favour the beacons marking the channels. **White-fronted Terns (43)** are common, **Caspian Terns (41)** less so, and **Black-fronted Terns (43)** have been reported. **Southern Black-backed Gulls (27, 34, 40)** and **Silver Gulls** are all numerous about the harbour and the **Black-billed Gull (29, 38)** is seen occasionally.

Cape Town to the Persian Gulf

The sea area around the Cape of Good Hope in latitude 34°S. lies within the oceanic zone of the albatrosses, shearwaters and petrels which sweep across the southern latitudes of the Atlantic and Indian Oceans. In these latitudes they are present at all seasons of the year, a proportion of albatrosses always being seen in immature plumage, but numbers are reinforced during the southern winter months, particularly between May and September. Pintado Petrels and prions are to be seen at times north of the Tropic of Capricorn, dispersing to these latitudes to a greater extent off the west coast of Africa than the east coast.

The gulls and terns most likely to be seen in Table Bay are described in Route 7.

During the early part of the route until past Durban the ship will be well within the offshore range of the **Cape Gannet (18)**, very similar indeed at first sight to the Northern Gannet but with primaries, secondaries and tail feathers blackish-brown.

Many different species of oceanic seabirds may now be in view in the course of one forenoon or afternoon. The variety is so great that no better example can be given than to pick out from a plethora of seabird plots those likely to be seen while rounding the Cape of Good Hope at the peak period between May and October.

This is perhaps the time for an advance study of the descriptions in the list which follows. One may ask at this stage which will most probably be seen; the following is an attempt to suggest an answer.

Prions

ALBATROSSES: **Wandering Albatross (3), Yellow-nosed** and **Black-browed Albatrosses (5), Sooty Albatross (6), Shy Albatross (4).**

SHEARWATERS: **Sooty Shearwater (8).**

PETRELS: **White-chinned Petrel (7), Giant Petrel (6, 7),** Pintado Petrel and **prions (11), Soft-plumaged, Grey-faced** and **Schlegel's Petrels (10).**

OTHER SPECIES: southern **Great Skua (26).**

The above list omits certain species which are more likely to be seen outside the months quoted such as **Wilson's Storm-petrel (13), Great** and **Cory's Shearwaters (9), Pomarine Skua (26), Arctic Tern (41, 42).**

After rounding the Cape of Good Hope the route passes sufficiently close to the coast as far as Durban for the Cape Gannet to be seen. At this time of the year the Wandering Albatross, Yellow-nosed and Black-browed Albatrosses, White-chinned Petrel, Pintado Petrel and prions will continue to be seen, but in decreasing numbers, until reaching the Tropic of Capricorn. A lookout should also be kept for the Soft-plumaged Petrel which occurs on the route during the southern winter months. Wilson's Storm-petrels have also been seen both in spring and autumn passing through the Mozambique Channel.

From Durban onwards, the route passes up the centre of the Mozambique Channel at too great a distance from the coast for coastal gulls and terns to be seen. The **Sooty Tern (44)** and **Crested Tern (41)** may occur, but it will not be until the ship approaches the Comoro Is. that the tropical seabirds will really become evident. From here onwards Sooty Terns become more plentiful; **Red-tailed** and **White-tailed Tropic-birds (15), Blue-faced Boobies (18)** and **Red-footed Boobies (19),** and **Great** and **Lesser Frigate-birds (24)** may all be seen occasionally, for their main breeding islands lie at some distance to the eastward. It is possible that **Pomarine Skuas (26)** follow a migratory route along the east coast of Africa for species have been observed between Durban and the south coast of Malagasy, and they are known to pass across the Persian Gulf on migration.

North of 10°S. a lookout should be kept for **Audubon's Shearwater (9).** This small sturdy shearwater with rich dark brown upperparts and white underparts may be

Audubon's Shearwater

seen flying with a rapid flutter of several wing-beats and short glides. It has only been reported occasionally. During the southern winter months **White-bellied Storm-petrels (13)** disperse northwards and cross the Equator into the N. Indian Ocean. They have been observed occasionally on the route north of the Equator in June and July. It is possible that **Black-bellied Storm-petrels (13)** may also occur. Both species are almost identical and it is difficult to distinguish between them at sea.

Onwards towards Socotra I. similar seabirds are likely to be seen. Thereafter a new pattern of seabirds will emerge, described in detail at the conclusion of Route 9 and in Route 10.

Singapore to Cape Town

The route covered from Singapore to Cape Town passes east of Bangka I., through the Sunda Strait, thence by Great Circle route north of the Cocos Keeling Is. to approximately 30°S., 60°E. and onwards towards the Cape of Good Hope.

At the opening stages of the passage and until clear of the Sunda Strait many tropical seabirds occur and an observer would be unlucky if he did not sight **Blue-faced Boobies (18)**, **Brown** and **Red-footed Boobies (19)**, **Great** and **Lesser Frigate-birds (24)**, **White-tailed** and **Red-tailed Tropic-birds (15)** and **Sooty Terns (44)**. Considerable numbers of Lesser Frigate-birds have been observed in the vicinity of Saja I.

It is less likely that any storm-petrel will be sighted. However it is known that a certain number of **Swinhoe's Storm-petrels (14)** pass through the Malacca Strait from the China Sea and at the very outset of the voyage this possibility should not be overlooked. Swinhoe's Storm-petrel can be identified by its dark rump, overall dark sooty-brown plumage, short legs, forked tail and distinctive bounding and swooping flight, lacking the weaker pattering flight of many other storm-petrels. Less likely also will be the sight of a **Pomarine Skua (26)**. Pomarine Skuas have been observed however both in the spring in April and again in the late autumn and winter in the vicinity of Singapore, while others have been observed at these seasons east of the Philippine Is. and New Guinea, presumably following a migratory route where they have been observed east of Japan to and from their breeding areas in the northern tundra of eastern Russia.

On entering the Indian Ocean individual species of the tropical seabirds already mentioned will still be seen. Sooty Terns, White-tailed and Red-tailed Tropic-birds and Red-footed Boobies tend to range at a greater distance from the land. On closing and passing the Cocos Keeling Is. a noticeable increase in seabirds will become apparent, but during the passage towards the islands a lookout should be kept for the appearance of two Indian Ocean shearwaters, the **Wedge-tailed Shearwater (7)** and the **Pale-footed Shearwater (8)**. The Wedge-tailed Shearwater spreads widely across the Indian Ocean north of the Tropic of Capricorn where it occurs in its dark phase. It breeds on the Cocos Keeling Is. and on the Chagos, Rodriguez, Mauritius, Reunion, Cargados, Carajos, Amirantes and Seychelles Is. in the central and western areas of the N. Indian Ocean. In appearance it is a medium sized lightly built shearwater with long broadish wings, dark chocolate-brown above with brownish-grey underparts, a long slender grey bill and markedly long wedge-shaped tail. It flies with a freer swooping and shearwatering flight than the Pale-footed Shearwater. The Pale-footed Shearwater of the Indian Ocean breeds on islands off S.W. Australia and migrates north of the Equator in the southern winter, commencing its journey in May and may be expected to be seen at this stage of the voyage in late May and June and again on return in October.

In appearance it is a heavily built uniformly chocolate-brown shearwater with long moderately slender wings, a short round tail, noticeably massive long pale bill with a dark tip and flesh-coloured legs. Its flight is slower and more laboured than that of the Wedge-tailed Shearwater, making use of slower wing-beats and glides.

Blue-faced Booby and Sooty Tern

The Cocos Keeling Islands

The following seabirds are known to breed on the islands: Wedge-tailed Shearwater, Red-tailed Tropic-bird, White-tailed Tropic-bird, Blue-faced Booby, Red-footed Booby (very large numbers), Brown Booby, Great Frigate-bird (large numbers), Lesser Frigate-bird (large numbers), Sooty Tern, **Common Noddy (44)**, and **White Tern (43)**. Wedge-tailed Shearwaters, Red-tailed Tropic-birds, Red-footed Boobies and Great Frigate-birds have been seen regularly by ships passing the islands, the latter two species sometimes in large groups. It is not uncommon for Red-footed Boobies to alight on ships. Other species may well be seen the closer that a ship passes the islands.

The mid-ocean passage

The central portion of the Indian Ocean passage lies outside the range of all but the most oceanic species, and at the best only chance encounters with Wedge-tailed and Pale-footed Shearwaters are likely during the first half of the passage. Three or possibly four storm-petrels occur however which migrate north of the Equator during the southern winter.

Wilson's Storm-petrels (13) breed in the sub-antarctic islands including Kerguelen and Heard Is. and migrate in large numbers northwards through the Indian Ocean

Wilson's Storm-petrel and Lesser Frigate Bird

arriving at their favoured feeding areas off the Arabian coast in June and commencing their return journey towards the end of October. This is the only all dark storm-petrel with a white rump patch to be seen in the Indian Ocean, and with its square tail, exceedingly long legs (the webs of its feet project beyond its tail when extended in flight), and habit of following in the wake of ships, cannot be confused with other species. **White-faced Storm-petrel (13)**. These breed on the south-western and southern coasts of Australia and migrate northwards through the Indian Ocean to arrive in the northern quarter of the Indian Ocean and Arabian Sea in July, leaving on their return journey about September. This is a very distinctive storm-petrel with brown upperwings and lower back, greyish-brown crown, nape and upper back, and grey upper tail-coverts which contrast with its white face, underparts and underwing-coverts. A dark patch shows below the eye. In flight it swings from side to side, glides on stiff wings and often dangles its legs.

It is known that the remaining two storm-petrels, the **White-bellied** and **Black-bellied Storm-petrels (13)**, penetrate northwards and cross the Equator in the Indian Ocean during the southern winter, their numbers appearing limited from present observations. The difficulty in positive identification lies in the variation in the white underbody plumage which occurs in both species. The Black-bellied species normally has a dark line of feathers dividing the centre of the white underbody but this is sometimes absent in the palest birds, while the normal entirely white underbody of the White-bellied species is sometimes streaked. The relatively few birds seen chiefly in the Arabian Sea area between July and September by independent observers have been reported as the White-bellied species. One specimen of the Black-bellied species in the British Museum (Natural History) is labelled 'Indian Ocean', and a good drawing of another seen in the central Arabian Sea is known.

The latter half of the passage

On passing south of the Tropic of Capricorn (23.5°S.), the ship will be entering the zone in which albatrosses and petrels common to the southern oceans may be expected to appear. In the early stages it may well be a **White-chinned Petrel (7)** that will be observed following the ship. This large heavily built black petrel with broad wings is best identified by its long massive pale bill but also shows a white patch on the chin. **Wandering Albatrosses (3)** will soon be seen. In the southern winter months they have been recorded as far north as the Tropic of Capricorn and throughout the whole year from 50°S. A lookout should also be kept for **Yellow-nosed Albatrosses (5)** which breed on Amsterdam and St Paul Is.

Now more species may begin to appear. The **Sooty Albatross (6)**, **Soft-plumaged Petrel (10)** and **Broad-billed Prion** (p. 47) also breed on Amsterdam and St Paul Is. and may be seen at this stage. The uniformly dark Sooty Albatross should not be mistaken for the **Light-mantled Sooty Albatross (6)** which ranges considerably further south. At close range look for a yellow line on the lower mandible of the Sooty Albatross. The medium sized Soft-plumaged Petrel is recognisable by its ash-grey upperparts, white forehead and face and underbody with mottled sides, and especially by its dark underwing-coverts. Its flight is usually fast and erratic, wings sharply angled. It may have been seen earlier in the passage and should not be confused with the White-faced Storm-petrel if the underwings are seen to be dark.

South of Malagasy and as the ship approaches the southern tip of S. Africa, the number and variety of seabirds will increase steadily. **Black-browed Albatrosses (5)**, **Grey-faced** and **Brown Petrels (10)**, **Pintado Petrels (11)**, **Giant Petrels (6, 7)** and prions may be seen.

It seems possible that Wilson's Storm-petrels and Pomarine Skuas follow a migratory route up and down the east coast of Africa during migration for both species have been observed on the east coast and between Durban and the south coast of Malagasy in November, the latter passing across the Persian Gulf in May/June.

The Brown Petrel and Great-winged Petrel are certainly less likely to be seen than the White-chinned Petrel. The Brown Petrel is another large heavily built species with long broad wings, brownish-grey above with pale grey face and neck, white underbody and greyish-brown underwing-coverts. It has a long thick greenish bill. Known by seamen as the "Cape Dove", it also follows ships with flapping and gliding flight. The Great-winged Petrel is of medium size, of overall dark brown colour showing a grey patch around its short stout black bill. Unlike the White-chinned and Brown Petrels, its flight is swift and free, banking high above the sea with its very long wings bent at the wrists.

The ship will now be approaching the southern coast of S. Africa where **Cape Gannets (18)** and **Southern Black-backed Gulls (27, 34, 40)** may be seen, and the seabirds to be seen during the last stages of the passage are described in Route 12.

Cape Town to Fremantle

The main portion of this long sea passage lies in mid latitude 32°S., passing some 400 miles north of Amsterdam and St Paul Is. Records from observers in the mid-ocean sector, although not numerous, confirm the presence of certain species.

On leaving Cape Town and until reaching longitude 40°E., the details of seabirds are included in Route 12. Thereafter the **Wandering Albatross (3)**, **Black-browed** and **Yellow-nosed Albatrosses (5)**, **White-chinned Petrel (7)**, **Grey-faced** and **Soft-plumaged Petrels (10)** and **Pintado Petrel (11)** may all be seen along the route. It is probable however that during the main portion of the passage only intermittent sightings will occur.

In addition to the above, isolated sightings of the **Brown Petrel (10)**, **White-headed Petrel (11)**, **Wilson's**, **Black-bellied** and **White-bellied Storm-petrels (13)**, and flocks of prions have been reported during the southern winter months.

Yellow-nosed and Black-browed Albatrosses

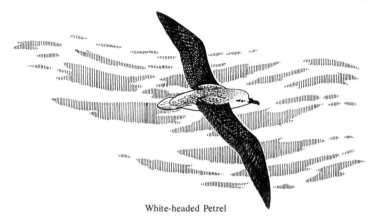

White-headed Petrel

Apart from the albatrosses, the Pintado Petrel, White-chinned Petrel and Brown Petrel are regular ship followers, and will be distinguished most easily. The Grey-faced Petrel, Soft-plumaged Petrel and White-headed Petrel pay no attention to ships. The White-chinned and Brown Petrels are large heavily built species, normally employing steady flaps and long glides in flight. On the other hand, the Grey-faced, White-headed and Soft-plumaged Petrels tend to swoop and soar in high arcs above sea level, particularly in the strong winds prevailing in these latitudes.

Wilson's Storm-petrels undertake a great northerly migration during the southern winter, crossing the Equator in the Indian Ocean and reaching the Arabian Sea at approximately the end of May and starting their return journey in October. They are known to follow certain routes, but the breadth of their dispersion in mid-ocean is unknown. During late March and April, and again in October and November they may be expected along the route, often following in the wake, their particularly long legs dangling as they flutter in search of minute marine organisms. Much less is known of the movements of the White-bellied and Black-bellied Storm-petrels, both so similar that positive identification at sea is extremely difficult. That both species disperse northwards into similar areas to the Wilson's Storm-petrel is recognised, but only a few have been reported. They tend to hop and flutter along the surface when feeding.

As the ship approaches the coast of Western Australia the numbers of seabirds will increase, and further details will be found in Route 11.

Fremantle Harbour

In Fremantle harbour, **Silver Gulls (29, 38, 40)** will greet the ship. These attractive white gulls with grey mantles, a large white spot showing near the tips of the leading black primaries, and red bills and legs, are usually abundant. The much larger **Pacific Gull (27, 34, 40)** differs from the Southern Black-backed Gull of New Zealand by its black tail band and heavier bill. The **Pied** and **Little Pied Cormorants (22)** and **Australian Pelican (17)** may be seen, and **Crested** and **Caspian Terns (42)**, and **Fairy Terns (43)** have all been recorded by ships.

ROUTE 15

Japan to Aden

The route from Yokohama passes to the eastward of the south islands of Japan, thence south of Taiwan, through the China Sea and Malacca Strait, emerging into the Bay of Bengal south of the Nicobar Is. and onwards south of Sri Lanka. From here the route passes north of the Maldive Is. and so direct to Aden.

On leaving Yokohama and apart from those coastal species quoted in Route 19, **White-faced Shearwaters (8)**, extremely plentiful in summer months often in large flocks, **Bonin Petrels (12)**, **Wedge-tailed Shearwaters (7)** and **Bulwer's Petrels (9)** have been seen on the route at all seasons. In winter perhaps a few **Common Kittiwakes (33, 39)** may occur, probably no further south than the 30th parallel.

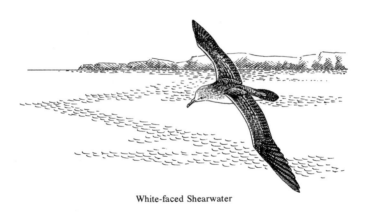

White-faced Shearwater

The China Sea

As the passage passes onwards through the China Sea, White-faced and Wedge-tailed Shearwaters are still to be seen at all seasons, and one species of storm-petrel, **Swinhoe's Storm-petrel (14)** occurs but has been recorded rarely. This is a relatively small species, sooty-brown above with paler upperwing-coverts, sooty-grey underparts and a slightly forked tail. It is now known to disperse also westwards across the N. Indian Ocean where a few specimens have been observed; any further reports of its occurrence in the Indian Ocean would be very valuable. The route soon enters the zone of the tropical seabirds. **Blue-faced Boobies (18)**, **Brown Boobies (19)** and **Sooty Terns (44)** are seen more frequently than other species, although **Brown-winged** or **Bridled Terns (44)** and **White-tailed Tropic-birds (15)** may also be seen.

MIGRANT PHALAROPES AND SKUAS. **Pomarine Skuas (26)** have been reported by ships on several occasions in the China Sea and Malacca Strait, and it seems

78

Bridled Tern

probable that these skuas follow a route through the China and East China Seas and Sea of Japan during migrations. They have been reported in April, October and on occasion in January. Some may winter off the south coast of Western Australia where isolated sightings have occurred in January and April.

The area off the north coast of New Guinea is a favourite wintering area for **Red-necked Phalaropes (25)**, which, like the Pomarine Skuas, breed far north in arctic regions. These little waders have been recorded once or twice by ships both in October and February in flocks east of Taiwan.

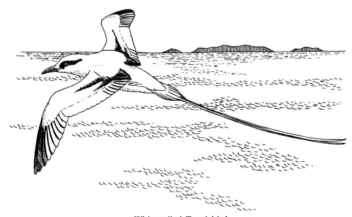

White-tailed Tropicbird

Southwards to the Malacca Strait

On approaching Singapore past the tropical islands at the southern end of the China Sea the **Great** and **Lesser Frigate-birds (24)** will be seen in addition to boobies, Sooty and Brown-winged Terns and tropic-birds. Swinhoe's Storm-petrel has been observed occasionally. There is likely to be little change in the Malacca Strait and while passing north of Sumatra.

The Bay of Bengal and tropical Indian Ocean

The passage now covers a warm water belt where sightings of seabirds are usually infrequent. Wedge-tailed Shearwaters and Sooty Terns are seen. In June and July and again between August and October however, **Wilson's Storm-petrels (13)** have occurred frequently between Sumatra and the west coast of southern India. The area of spread of the vast numbers of Wilson's Storm-petrels which migrate into the northern part of the Indian Ocean in the early summer from their breeding quarters in the sub-antarctic and antarctic is imperfectly known. That they converge towards the western sector of the Arabian Sea and congregate in thousands in offshore waters from the Gulf of Oman to the Gulf of Aden between June and late September is abundantly clear. Numbers undoubtedly pass up the west coast of India, and some probably past Madagascar (Malagasy), and they will be seen at these seasons as the ship enters the Gulf of Aden. The **Pale-footed Shearwater (8)** also migrates into the N. Indian Ocean in the summer. This heavily built species with a uniform chocolate-brown plumage is most easily distinguished from the dark phase Wedge-tailed Shearwater, which occurs in the Indian Ocean, by the difference in the colour of the bill and shape of the tail. The Pale-footed Shearwater has a conspicuous long straw-coloured bill with a dark tip and short round tail. The bill of the Wedge-tailed species is long, more slender and grey and its tail noticeably long and wedge-shaped. The Pale-footed Shearwaters which cross the Equator breed on islands off S.W. Australia and appear to sweep northwards towards Sri Lanka, and so in an anti-clockwise direction into the western sector of the Arabian Sea where they arrive about June. They commence their return journey from the end of September onwards, and may well spread across the central portion of the Indian Ocean as they move southwards.

Sri Lanka to Aden: the Maldive and Laccadive Islands

Although a number of tropical seabirds including **Audubon's Shearwater (9)** have been reported breeding amongst the islands, very few are likely to be seen on the passage. Such species as the Black-naped Tern, the White Tern, Common Noddy and Lesser Noddy keep close to the islands and have not been reported by ships. Indeed if any seabirds other than shearwaters are to be seen they are likely to be Sooty Terns, Brown-winged Terns, or the occasional **Red-billed Tropic-bird (15)** and Lesser Frigate-bird.

From the Maldive Is. onwards, once again sightings will be chancy, the occasional Red-billed Tropic-bird, Sooty Tern or Wedge-tailed Shearwater. On this latter part of the voyage however the opportunity may arise of sighting **White-faced**, **White-bellied** and **Black-bellied Storm-petrels (13)**. Like the Wilson's Storm-petrel, these species also undertake similar northerly and southerly migrations, moving north of the Equator during the southern winter, probably on a broader front. Neither have been seen in large numbers, indeed only occasionally on the route, and usually singly or in pairs. They are very different in appearance and flight characteristics. The most distinctive features of the White-faced Storm-petrel are the greyish head, neck, back and tail-coverts set against the brown upperwings, the totally white underparts and, most distinctive of all, the white face with its dusky eye patch. It does not follow ships. The White-bellied Storm-petrel on the other hand has sooty-black upperparts, a white patch above the rump and a white underbelly – it tends to follow ships and hops and flutters with legs drooped with a weak butterfly appearance. It may be also that the very similar Black-bellied Storm-petrel also crosses the Equator in like manner; the Black-bellied species is similar but normally shows a thin black line of feathers down the centre of its belly, but not always! It is the White-bellied species however that has been reported with greater certainty along the route.

    Little more can be said of this passage across the tropical Indian Ocean, which can often be extremely disappointing to the birdwatcher, until the ship approaches the Gulf of Aden. At this stage the traveller should turn to Route 9 wherein the seabirds are described.

ROUTE 16

Hong Kong to Fremantle

The route passes across the north end of the South China Sea, through the Sulu and Celebes Seas, the Strait of Makassar, the Lombok Strait, thence southwards towards the North West Cape of Australia and onwards to Fremantle.

Leaving harbour

The **Northern Black-headed Gull (28, 31, 32, 37, 40)**, the **Herring Gull (28, 35, 40)** and occasionally the **Japanese Gull (27, 34)** visit the harbour in winter months. In summer months a variety of terns may be seen on the marshes, of which the **Whiskered** and **White-winged Black Terns (44)**, **Caspian Tern (42)**, **Gull-billed** and **Little Terns (43)** have been reported, but these terns are unlikely to be seen by a ship leaving harbour. The **Common Cormorant (20)** occurs in the approaches to harbours.

The China Sea

During the passage of the China Sea **White-faced Shearwaters (8)** are likely to be seen frequently. These breed on islands off Japan, the Izu and Pescadore Is.,

Bulwer's Petrel

82

migrate southwards during the northern winter, and are thus more frequent at this season. A lookout should be kept for **Wedge-tailed Shearwaters (7)**. These breed on the Bonin and Volcano Is. where they occur in the pale phase. The much smaller uniformly sooty-brown **Bulwer's Petrel (9)**, which breeds on the same islands, also occurs. During a single passage the chance of sighting a storm-petrel is small. If one is sighted flying with a strong bounding flight and with an overall sooty-brown plumage, paler wing-coverts and a slightly forked tail (the latter difficult to discern), it will almost certainly be **Swinhoe's Storm-petrel (14)**. This breeds on the Pescadore Is. and moves southwards through the China Sea in winter. The very similar but slightly larger **Matsudaira's Storm-petrel (14)** breeds on the Volcano Is. and appears to winter normally southwards east of the Philippine Is. It can only be distinguished at very close range by whitish areas towards the outer ends of its wings due to white shafts to its primaries.

During early spring and late autumn an occasional **Pomarine Skua (26)** and little **Red-necked Phalaropes (25)** may be observed on migration, the latter to be seen later

Red-necked Phalarope

in the voyage in its wintering areas. Close to the Philippine Is. **Sooty Terns (44)** and **Brown Boobies (19)** are likely to occur.

As the ship proceeds through the Sulu Sea and beyond, an increasing variety of tropical seabirds will appear. **Sooty Terns (44)**, **Brown Boobies (19)** and **Red-footed Boobies (19)** are sure to be seen, adults in both the white and brown phases. Sooty Terns will be frequent. **White-tailed Tropic-birds (15)** and both the **Great** and **Lesser Frigate-birds (24)** are common in the area, although it is easy to be mistaken in differentiating between them at sea. In the late autumn and winter considerable flocks of Red-necked Phalaropes winter at sea both west of the Philippine Is. and indeed throughout the area as far as the Lombok Strait. They have been observed as late as April before migrating north. It is far less certain whether **Grey Phalaropes (25)** occur amongst them.

The Lombok Strait and beyond

After passing south of the Strait the **Red-tailed Tropic-bird (15)** and the golden-tinted plumage of the **Christmas Tropic-bird (15)**, a race of the White-tailed Tropic-bird, should be looked for. This race breeds on Christmas I. Brown

Boobies, Blue-faced Boobies, **Common Noddies (44)**, which may well have been seen earlier, and Sooty Terns may still be seen in the vicinity of the Lombok Strait.

As the voyage continues towards the North West Cape and beyond, both the Wedge-tailed Shearwater and, for the first time, the **Pale-footed Shearwater (8)** are likely to be seen. This large chocolate-brown shearwater, with its thick straw-coloured bill and dark tip, breeds on islands off S.W. Australia in the southern summer and migrates northwards in an anti-clockwise sweep, crossing the Equator to reach the Arabian Sea by July. Both species are seen regularly on the route. The **Soft-plumaged Petrel (10)**, whose nearest breeding island is St Paul in the mid S. Indian Ocean, has been seen on occasions north-west of North West Cape but more frequently further south and west. Its white face, dark eye patch, slate-grey back, dark brown upperwings and grey breast band to its whitish underbody, and in particular its dark underwings, distinguish it. Its flight is fast and erratic.

Southwards towards Fremantle

As the ship approaches the Tropic of Capricorn (23.5°S.), it enters the zone of the northern limit of certain southern ocean species. The first albatross will appear, most probably the **Yellow-nosed Albatross (5)**. Thereafter southern ocean petrels will occur in increasing variety. Perhaps a large broadwinged black species with a long massive whitish bill will be seen following astern with steady flaps and glides. A closer view may show some white under its chin. This will surely be the **White-chinned Petrel (7)**. Later a medium sized brownish-grey petrel with a short black hooked bill and long narrow wings, flying in fast high banked arcs, will prove to be the **Grey-faced Petrel (10)**. Off the coast the **Little Shearwater (9)** which breeds off the west coast of S.W. Australia may be seen. Very small in size, appearing black above with white underparts and underwings, it is seen flying low over the sea with a series of very rapid stiff wing-beats and short glides.

Before reaching 30°S., **Wandering Albatrosses (3)** and **Pintado Petrels (11)** are likely to be following the ship, and the first **Giant Petrel (6, 7)** and southern **Great Skua (26)** may appear. Flocks of small **prions (11)** may add to the scene.

The approaches to Fremantle

A lookout should be kept for the **Crested Tern (42)** which ranges at some distance to seaward. In the approach to harbour **Silver Gulls (29, 38, 40)** may greet the ship. Here the much larger **Pacific Gull (27, 34, 40)** differs from the Southern Black-backed Gull of New Zealand by its heavier build and bill and the black band on its white tail. The **Pied** and **Little Pied Cormorants (22)**, Crested Tern, **Caspian Tern (42)**, and **Fairy Tern (43)** have been recorded and the **Australian Pelican (17)** may be seen.

Hong Kong to the Bass Strait

The route described after crossing the South China Sea passes west of the Philippine Is., east of the eastern tip of Celebes, between Ceram and Buru Is., onwards to the Torres Strait, past the Great Barrier Reef and thence off the coast of Queensland and New South Wales to the Bass Strait. Probably a greater variety of tropical seabirds may be seen than in any other sea area, added to which the latter part of the route enters the area of the albatrosses and petrels common to the southern oceans. Many of the same species are likely to be seen again and again, and it is only possible throughout the tropical zone to quote a general list of species in no particular order as the passage proceeds.

Leaving harbour

The seabirds in the vicinity of Hong Kong and during the passage of the China Sea are described in Route 16.

West of the Philippine Is. and onwards

At the outset White-faced Shearwaters will continue to be seen during late autumn and winter but are unlikely to occur south of the Philippines. A whole host of tropical seabirds, some of which may have occurred earlier, are now liable to be seen until passing through the Torres Strait, and may be summarised as follows:

White-tailed Tropic-bird (15), **Red-footed** and **Brown Boobies (19)**, common throughout the islands. The Red-footed Booby is likely to be more prevalent in the vicinity of the Philippine Is. and may occur in both the adult white and brown phases. **Great** and **Lesser Frigate-birds (24)**, the latter occurring more frequently. **Sooty** and **Brown-winged** or **Bridled Terns (44)**. Both species have been observed but in greater numbers in the vicinity of the Philippine Is. **Crested** and **Lesser-crested Terns (41)**. Here again the Crested Tern has been observed more frequently among the Philippine Is., while the Lesser-crested Tern commonly south of New Guinea and beyond. The **Little Tern (43)** has been observed once or twice and may stray into the area from the northern coast of Australia. **Common** or **Brown** and **White-capped Noddies (44)**. Both species occur, they tend to remain close to islands and few observations are available. **Wilson's Storm-petrel (13)**. The migratory movements of these storm-petrels in the western Pacific are not entirely clear. There is however a positive record along the route on 9th September 1969, at 4°53'S., 134°07'E., near the Aroe Is. south of New Guinea, of 60 Wilson's Storm-petrels flying close alongside a ship for 15 minutes. This dark storm-petrel, with a paler band on the upperwing-coverts, square tail, white rump patch and legs peeping beyond the tail in flight, could have been no other species. They may be seen in sea areas north of Australia as winter visitors.

PHALAROPES. The area between N. Borneo and New Guinea is a favourite wintering area for **Red-necked Phalaropes (25)**. Large flocks have been seen west of the Philippines as early as August which would appear to be an unusually early date

Common Noddy

for their arrival. Other flocks have been seen in January and again in April, the birds doubtless congregating during the latter month at the season of their northwards migrations. Large numbers have also been observed wintering as far south as the Lombok Strait.

SKUAS. **Pomarine Skuas (26)** undoubtedly pass through the South China Sea on migration and also to the east of the Philippines and New Guinea and have been observed also to the west of the Philippines.

The Torres Strait to the Capricorn

The Wedge-tailed Shearwater, seen earlier in the South China Sea, is now likely to be seen regularly. Within the Torres Strait, Brown Boobies, Lesser Frigate-birds, **White-capped Noddies (44)**, Crested and Lesser-crested Terns and Sooty Terns, and a newcomer, the **Silver Gull (29, 38, 40)**, may be seen. It is the only small gull breeding in Australia, and with its grey upperparts, white underparts, broad white patch near the tip of its leading primary and red bill and legs is easily identified.

The Great Barrier Reef

Many species breed on islets and cays to seaward of the Great Barrier Reef and also close along the coastline of Queensland. Not all may be seen along the sea route, but the following list of species breeding in this area includes the majority that have been sighted: Wedge-tailed Shearwater, Great Frigate-bird, Lesser Frigate-bird, Brown Booby, Blue-faced Booby, Red-footed Booby, Red-tailed Tropic-bird, Crested Tern, Sooty Tern, Common or Brown Noddy. Closer to the coast, Silver Gulls, **Pied Cormorants (22)** and **Australian Pelicans (17)** have all been observed.

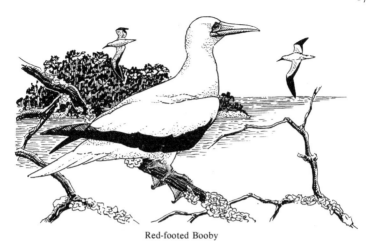

Red-footed Booby

The Tropic of Capricorn and beyond

During the southern winter months, broadly from June to September, numbers of southern spring and summer breeding albatrosses, shearwaters and petrels disperse northwards into more temperate latitudes, certain shearwaters undertaking an extensive migration even earlier into high latitudes in the N. Pacific, to return to their breeding quarters by November.

Even before reaching the Tropic of Capricorn, one may expect to sight some of these species during the southern winter. The first albatross to be seen is likely to be a **Wandering Albatross (3)**, often in immature plumage. South of 30°S. for the remainder of the voyage these albatrosses may well be accompanying the ship daily. It has been found that large numbers of these birds congregate close off the coast of New South Wales between May and November to feed off refuse where they have been caught in nets and banded. Recoveries of some banded birds have occurred thousands of miles away on breeding grounds in S. Georgia. **Pintado Petrels (11)**. These unmistakable piebald birds which often follow ships in flocks have been seen at 23°S. in August, but are not normally seen regularly until south of 30°S.

We must now turn to three shearwaters which undertake the great trans-equatorial migrations, the **Short-tailed, Sooty** and **Pale-footed Shearwaters (8)**. The Short-tailed and Sooty Shearwaters are the "Mutton Birds" of the Bass Strait and New Zealand respectively where they breed in abundance. On completion of the breeding season adults and young sweep northwards to the east of Australia in early May. Sometimes large flocks may be seen on the route south of the latitude of Capricorn from May onwards and again in October, the greater proportion likely to be Short-tailed Shearwaters. The Pale-footed Shearwater, which breeds both in New Zealand and Lord Howe I., undertakes a very similar migration and has also been seen although the majority appear to migrate further to the eastward. Short-tailed and Sooty Shearwaters are very similar and may easily be confused at sea. The Sooty is larger with a longer slender dark grey bill, sometimes showing a pale patch on the chin, but most easily distinguished by the silvery appearance of its underwing compared with the greyish underwing of the Short-tailed species. The **Grey-backed Shearwater (8)** which also breeds in New Zealand migrates north of the Equator well to the eastward of the route.

It would be impossible to be categorical as to the total variety of petrels and shearwaters ranging in the ocean to the east of Australia on dispersal from their breeding quarters and which may appear on the route. It is certain that in the region of 30°S. in September there are records of **Kermadec** and **Gould's Petrels (12)**, **Common Diving-petrels (14)** and **Fluttering Shearwaters (10)**, close off the coast of New South Wales. Kermadec Petrels might be confused with **Solander's Petrel (12)**, both of which breed on Lord Howe I. Solander's Petrel is larger, general greyish-brown above and below and with a freer banking and swooping flight. The Kermadec Petrel is darker brown above with a very variable whitish to brownish underbody. Both species have dark brown underwings with distinctive white oval patches, the white patches in the Kermadec closer to the wing tips.

Gould's Petrels also breed on Cabbage Tree I. off New South Wales but are much smaller, lightly built gadfly petrels showing a dark inverted W pattern on medium-grey upperwings, white underparts with dark margins to white underwings. Common Diving-petrels are easily recognised by their very small size, stubby black and white bodies and habit of diving, while the brown-backed Fluttering Shearwaters with their white underparts are often seen resting on the water or skimming low over the sea in rapid fluttering flight.

From the latitude of Brisbane southward more species will appear. If the ship is close to the coast Silver Gulls and, outside the breeding season, **Australian Gannets (18)** may be expected. The Australian Gannet breeds in thousands on Pinnacle Rock and elsewhere in the Bass Strait and spreads along the south coast of Australia from Brisbane to Fremantle. Wandering Albatrosses will be joined by **Black-browed Albatrosses (5)** and **Shy Albatrosses (4)**. The Shy Albatross breeds on Albatross I. in the Bass Strait and is the only albatross to breed in Australia. They have the reputation of being shy birds keeping clear of ships. **Yellow-nosed Albatrosses (5)**, which are a common sight west of Tasmania by ships crossing the Great Australian Bight, also spread into the Tasman Sea. South of 30°S., **Giant Petrels (6, 7)** will be seen joining with albatrosses in following the ship. These very large scavengers with none of the grace of the albatrosses, brownish-grey in adult plumage when feather pigmentation fades, but glossy-brown in immatures and notable by their outstandingly large heavy pale bills, will wrangle with albatrosses astern of a ship for any garbage thrown overboard. Another predator of the southern oceans, the southern **Great Skua (26)**, may be seen during the closing stage of the voyage. Similar in appearance to the Great Skua of the northern hemisphere these birds have a habit of settling on ships' masts or derricks.

No mention has yet been made of smaller oceanic birds which may appear. Flocks of **Fairy Prions** (p. 000) spread northwards from their breeding quarters in the Bass Strait and New Zealand from February onwards, and have been observed as far north as the Tropic of Capricorn in August. It is the smallest of the different races, but very similar in its bluish-grey upperparts, showing a dark inverted W pattern across the wing, dark eye patch, white underparts and a distinctive black bar at the tip of the tail. The **White-faced Storm-petrel (13)** breeds on islands off the coast of Australia and New Zealand. This small storm-petrel with its distinctive plumage, which in the local race shows a dark rump, dances from side to side over the sea, sometimes hopping over the water or planing in a zigzag manner.

The Bass Strait

The islands in the Bass Strait provide a focal point and breeding area for many species; those large oceanic species already mentioned, the albatrosses, Giant Petrel, and southern Great Skua; Short-tailed Shearwaters in enormous numbers during their breeding season; Pintado Petrels and Fairy Prions; Australian Gannets, Silver Gulls and the large **Pacific Gull (27, 34, 40)**; Crested Terns and **Fairy Terns (43)**. Other species there are too, the Australian race of the **Common Cormorant (20, 23)**, the Pied Cormorant, **Little Pied Cormorant (22, 23)**, and the **Little Penguin (2)**, the only penguin breeding along the southern portion of Australia and coasts of Tasmania.

San Francisco to Guam

The route chosen covers a wide belt of open ocean far removed from islands, passing broadly between 40°N. and 30°N. until reaching the meridian of 180°, thence south-westwards entering the tropical belt east of Marcus I. and finally closing the Marianas Is. to arrival at Guam.

Only the most oceanic seabirds are likely to be seen over the majority of the passage together with a chance sighting of trans-oceanic migrants passing to and from arctic or southern ocean breeding areas.

San Francisco harbour and coastline

Numbers of inshore and offshore seabirds may be seen, some at all seasons, others on passage or wintering from more distant breeding areas. Close inshore the gulls will attract attention first. The **Western Gull (27, 34)** is a conspicuous resident coastal gull, more common in the inner reaches of harbour in autumn and winter. Its dark grey mantle and flesh-coloured legs distinguish it from the medium-grey mantle and greenish-yellow legs of the **California Gull (28, 35)**. The California Gull breeds largely on inland lakes, occurring more often on the coasts in autumn and winter. The local race of the **Herring Gull (28, 35, 40)** is very similar to the California Gull except for its pinkish legs. Breeding northwards from British Columbia it occurs at times as far south as San Francisco. The **Common** and **Ring-billed Gulls (28, 35, 40)** are two similar but distinctly smaller gulls with light grey mantles and greenish-yellow slender bills and legs, the Ring-billed Gull distinguished by the black sub-terminal band across its bill. Both breed inland north of California but appear as partial migrants. Yet another gull, **Heermann's Gull (30, 38)**, is easily distinguished in adult plumage by its white head, red bill, but otherwise overall dark slate-grey appearance. It breeds southwards from the Gulf of California. Numbers however disperse northwards after the breeding season and may be seen on the shore line by the late summer and autumn. **Bonaparte's Gull (31, 36)** occurs on the coast occasionally to and from inland northern breeding areas from S.E. Alaska and is more likely to be seen in early May and on return in late August.

The most striking migratory gull which passes down the Pacific coastline from its high arctic breeding area is the **Sabine's Gull (33, 39)**. Its distinctive grey, white and black triangular upperwing pattern and slightly forked white tail serve to distinguish it. In the autumn considerable numbers are sometimes seen off the coast, usually in more isolated numbers when northward bound in May and June. The **Glaucous-winged Gull (29, 35)**, which breeds from the Bering Sea south to Washington, also disperses southwards, often well out at sea, during the winter. Its large size and very pale appearance differ from all other gulls in the area.

CORMORANTS. These are a common sight in harbours perching on posts and seamarks as well as fishing off the coast. **Brandt's Cormorant (21)** is an abundant species. In the breeding season its throat pouch is blue but it is best distinguished at all seasons by the fawn coloured patch below the throat patch. Rafts of these birds may be seen well off the coast where small fish are shoaling. The **Pelagic Cormorant**

(21) is smaller and more graceful and may be distinguished by its smaller head, thin neck, slender bill, coral-red throat pouch, and, in breeding dress, by the white patch at the rear of each flank and crests on forehead and crown. The **Double-crested Cormorant (21)** carries an orange throat patch and tufts on each side of the head in breeding dress.

PELICANS. Both the very large **American White Pelican (17)**, which breeds largely on lakes in western Canada and N. America, and the smaller **Brown Pelican (17)**, which breeds on salt water coastlines, may be seen in harbour.

Leaving San Francisco harbour

It is not until a ship has cleared harbour and on the fringe of the open sea that the offshore seabirds are likely to be encountered. It is now that a lookout should be kept for certain species of the family Alcidae that may be seen at times at the outset of the voyage. Of these, **Cassin's Auklet (48)** is perhaps most abundant, often occurring well out at sea in winter. The plumage of this extremely small dusky-grey auklet blends so well with the grey sea that its presence may easily be overlooked. The **Pigeon Guillemot (46)** breeds locally along the coastline and may be seen at all seasons. In breeding plumage it is black overall showing a broad white wing patch divided by black transverse bars and bright red legs. In winter however its underparts are white and its upperparts show a very variable amount of white.

Much larger than the chunky auklets and murrelets, the **Tufted Puffin (47)** is easily recognised in breeding plumage by its black dress, enormous red bill, white cheeks and yellow plumes. In flight its bright red legs catch the eye.

The **Marbled Murrelet (48)**, a small chunky seabird, shows a considerable difference between its heavily barred and mottled-brownish breeding plumage and the slaty upperparts, white neck band and underparts in winter. It may be seen in either plumage although more probably in winter plumage. The **Ancient Murrelet (48)** is a winter visitor from its breeding areas in the Aleutian and Queen Charlotte Is. In winter plumage it appears slaty-grey above with white cheeks, throat, neck band and underparts. The **Rhinoceros Auklet (47)** is an irregular winter visitor from breeding areas in the Aleutian Is. south to Washington. This large auklet is more akin to puffins in size and structure. In winter plumage it appears sooty-black above with greyish-brown underparts and brownish bill lacking any horn at the base. It tends to range well out in the ocean.

The opening stage of the voyage

The first half of the voyage until the ship reaches the 'Date Line', 180° meridian, covers a north latitude belt in which there are likely to be considerable periods without sightings of seabirds. As will be seen later, this will depend to some extent upon the seasons at which the voyage takes place. However, the ship will not be entirely deserted, for from an early stage the **Black-footed Albatross (6)** is likely to pick up and follow the ship. Indeed these sooty-brown albatrosses, at times several in company, are likely to be seen regularly throughout the greater part of the voyage. They are always more numerous than **Laysan Albatrosses (4)** and bolder in approaching close astern of a ship. The Laysan Albatross does not appear to extend its range quite so close to the N. American coast. Both species breed on the Hawaiian Is. between October and July, dispersing northwards, but may be seen on the route at all seasons. A lookout should be kept at the outset for the small **Black-vented Shearwater (9)** which breeds on the west coast of Lower California from April onwards, dispersing northwards, and is more likely to be seen from late summer onwards. It appears sooty-black above, white below with black under tail-coverts and a noticeably long dark tail. In flight it normally proceeds with a series of quick wing-beats and glides. **Leach's Storm-petrel (13)** ranges westward along the route but has been reported rarely. Although normally showing a white rump patch divided centrally by a dark line of feathers, individuals in the area have been reported showing no trace of white above the rump, and could be mistaken for the **Tristram's Storm-petrel (14)**, likely to be seen at a later stage north of the Hawaiian Is.

Globe-spanning migrants; seasonal appearances

A number of species which either breed far south of the Equator or alternatively in high northern latitudes cross the path of the sea route at the appropriate seasons. During these periods they may be seen both close off the Pacific coastline at the outset of the voyage and also well out in the ocean. Here then a lookout should be kept for **Sooty** and **Pink-footed Shearwaters (8)**, **Red-necked** and **Grey Phalaropes (25)**, **Arctic**, **Pomarine** and **Long-tailed Skuas (26)**.

A full description of their seasonal movements off the coast of British Columbia with comments on identification at sea is included under Route 23 to which the reader is recommended to turn, the seasonal periods being equally applicable to the present route. See also Route 20.

The mid-ocean passage to 180° meridian

At all seasons, Black-footed Albatrosses and Laysan Albatrosses are likely to be seen daily, but otherwise seabirds are scarce. During the autumn and winter months on rare occasions the **Northern Fulmar (11)**, **Common Kittiwake (33, 39)** and **Fork-tailed Storm-petrel (14)** have been seen, species which breed in the Aleutian Is. but whose range southward during the winter is rarely south of 40°N. The Fork-tailed Storm-petrel is very distinctive, its pearly-grey upperparts, very pale grey underbody, dark underwings and forked tail being unlike any other storm-petrel.

If the voyage is taking place during October the observer should be on the alert for a sighting of **Short-tailed Shearwaters (8)** probably anywhere between 165°W. and 175°W. This species migrates northwards in the western quarter of the Pacific from its breeding areas in the Bass Strait and Tasmania to winter in high latitudes of the N. Pacific. Enormous flocks have been observed further south on southward migration flying south-west in the first week of November. If this movement is translated northwards to the area of the voyage the ship may cross the path of these dark shearwaters, distinguished from very similar Sooty Shearwaters by their smaller size and the darker under-surface of their wings. See also Route 19.

No mention has been made yet of the large and very rare **Short-tailed Albatross (3)** which was almost exterminated in the nineteenth century by feather hunting. Now there may be some 50 pairs breeding on Torishima I., south of Japan. It is reported to range northward and eastward. In adult plumage it is a white albatross with some dark markings on its upperwings, dark brown primaries and a dark tip to its tail.

Young chocolate-brown birds could easily be confused with the smaller Black-footed Albatross but show pale bills and legs. It keeps well clear of ships.

Southwards towards the Mariana Islands

From now onwards new species will appear on the scene. Black-footed and Laysan Albatrosses will remain for a while, plentiful to the west of Midway Is. The **Tristram's Storm-petrel (14)** may be seen for the first time. This is a large sooty-brown species with a long forked tail to be seen flying strongly compared with other storm-petrels in steep arcs, glides and fluttering wing-beats. **Bonin's Petrel (12)** breeds on the leeward Hawaiian chain and occurs frequently westward from the islands. This is a small 'gadfly' petrel with dark head, white forehead and cheeks, greyer back and upperwing-coverts, white underparts and wings with broad dark margins. Its bill is short, stout and black. Like other 'gadfly' petrels its flight is swift, swooping and banking.

The **Wedge-tailed Shearwater (7)**, a lightly built medium sized shearwater, is likely to be seen at intervals for the remainder of the passage, occurring in this area in the pale phase. Its long wedge-shaped tail and masterly shearwatering close to the sea is noticeable. It breeds on the leeward Hawaiian chain and Marianas Is. within the area of the route.

Throughout the islands in the tropical belt of the Pacific a great variety of seabirds other than truly oceanic species breed, but only a few range far out into the ocean. **Sooty Terns (44)** and **Red-tailed** and **White-tailed Tropic-birds (15)** are an exception and have been observed over 500 miles from land. These two species together with the **Common Noddy (44)** and **Red-footed Booby (19)** are known to breed on Marcus I. While the ship is still at some distance from Marcus I., the former two species may appear. There will be little difficulty identifying the Sooty Tern, nor the Red-tailed Tropic-bird if its blood-red tail streamers are seen. Immatures of this species however are similar to those of other tropic-birds showing dark speckling on the upperparts and lacking the elongated tail feathers. Tropic-birds are usually seen flying high overhead. The Common Noddy is unlikely to be seen at any distance

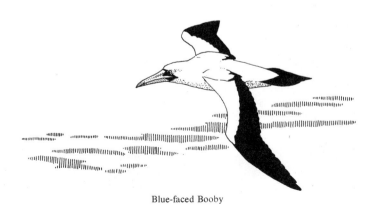

Blue-faced Booby

from the land; the Red-footed Booby on the other hand is frequently seen well out at sea, adults occurring both in the white and brown phase.

Sea areas to the west and north-west, in use by commercial shipping trading to and from Japan, have been well covered by oceanic seabird observations, but the latter part of the present route from 30°N. towards the Marianas remains a matter of speculation. Further westward the distribution maps show certain principal migration routes of the Sooty Shearwater, Short-tailed Shearwater, **Pale-footed Shearwater (8)**, and the main distribution areas of the **White-faced Shearwater (8)**, **Matsudaira's Storm-petrel (14)**, **Bulwer's Petrel (9)**, phalaropes and Pomarine Skuas. Indeed certain southern ocean 'gadfly' petrels which move into the N. Pacific outside their breeding seasons, such as the **Stejneger's**, **Peale's** and **Cook's Petrels (12)**, have been observed between 30° and 40°N. between Japan and 160°E. Thus the opportunity for sighting species at present unconfirmed along the present route provides interesting opportunities for future observers.

The Marianas

The islands provide breeding localities for many tropical seabirds. The Wedge-tailed Shearwater, Red-tailed Tropic-bird, Red-footed Booby and Sooty Tern may have been seen already. On approaching the islands other breeding species such as **Audubon's Shearwater (9)**, **White-tailed Tropic-bird (15)**, **Blue-faced Booby (18)**, and **Brown Booby (19)** may be seen at some distance to seaward. The **Common** and **White-capped Noddies (44)**, and the **White Tern (43)** tend to remain close off the islands. **Great Frigate-birds (24)**, **Crested Terns (42)** and **Black-naped Terns (43)** have been reported visiting the islands, and this list is surely not exhaustive; but as the ship enters Guam so the passage narrative must end.

White Tern

Panama to Japan

The route selected presupposes the Great Circle Track to the south of Hawaii, thence by Rhumb Line towards Midway I. and onwards by Great Circle to Yokohama.

Seabirds pay scant attention to such niceties of navigation; the presence of plankton, the confluence of contrasting cool and warm currents, the urges of migrations, it is on such bases that they restlessly wander over this wide ocean. The evidence of this narrative is based on day to day observations on a number of passages. The voyager may sight some species of shearwaters, more probably the 'Cookilaria' group of petrels, to which no reference is made, for as yet the seasonal range of many species is obscure.

Westwards from the Gulf of Panama

The seabirds likely to be seen to the longitude of 100°W. have been described in the concluding pages of Route 20. Our observations start from this point.

Boobies (18, 19) have been recorded to 110°W., **Red-billed Tropic-birds (15)** and **Sooty Terns (44)**, being more oceanic, as far as 120°W. From here onwards until reaching perhaps 150°W. it is the shearwaters, petrels and storm-petrels that are likely to cross the ship's path. On passing 100°W. the passage of **Sooty** and **Pink-footed Shearwaters (8)** quoted in Route 20 may still be expected, chiefly between May and July and again between late September and November. This belt between 100° and 110°W. appears also to be the extreme range at all seasons of the **Audubon's Shearwater (9)** from the Galapagos Is. Two further shearwaters are now likely to be seen, the larger (medium size) **Wedge-tailed Shearwater (7)**, to be seen with greater frequency as the passage proceeds, more usually in its pale phase, and the smaller **Black-vented Shearwater (9)** which breeds on the west coast of California. The Wedge-tailed Shearwater (pale phase) with chocolate-brown upperparts, white underparts, long slender pinkish bill and very noticeably long wedge-shaped tail is not difficult to identify. The Black-vented Shearwater on the other hand might well be confused with Audubon's Shearwater unless care is taken to study the descriptions carefully.

The **Hawaiian Petrel (12)** is prevalent in the area at all seasons from its breeding quarters on the Galapagos Is. and Hawaiian Is.

STORM-PETRELS. In this early part of the passage an observer is almost certain to notice storm-petrels and there are a variety at his disposal though these are extremely difficult to identify. To deal first with those which breed on the Galapagos Is. and the Pacific coast of tropical America: of these, the **Galapagos Storm-petrel (13)**, sooty-black with a triangular white rump patch, does not range far from its islands and is unlikely to be seen after passing 100°W. The commonest along the route to approximately 110°W. is likely to be the **Black Storm-petrel (14)**, which breeds on islands off Lower California, a much larger totally black storm-petrel, with a deeply forked tail. The **Leach's Storm-petrel (13)**, which has a large breeding range off the west coasts of Canada and N. America as far as Lower

California including Guadalupe I., ranges far to seawards and has been observed on several occasions, more frequently in the autumn. Smaller than the Black Storm-petrel, and also showing a forked tail at close quarters, it could be distinguished normally by the appearance of a white patch above the rump divided by some rather indistinct dusky feathers. The local race, however, may be seen equally as an all dark storm-petrel with little or no trace of white upper tail-coverts. The **Madeiran Storm-petrel (13)** breeds both on the Galapagos and Hawaiian Is. but does not appear to range to any distance from the islands. Its square tail and even broad white band across the rump helps to identify it.

One or two records have occurred of that very tiny all dark species, the **Least Storm-petrel (14)**, one specimen having been identified on board a ship. It breeds off Lower California. The Least Storm-petrel's very small size will help to establish its identity.

Onwards towards the Hawaiian islands

Wedge-tailed Shearwaters and Hawaiian Petrels are likely to be seen at intervals all the way to the Hawaiian Is., but between 130° and 150°W. little other seabird life is probable. From hereon seabirds local to the Hawaiian Is. should begin to appear. An occasional Sooty Tern and **Red-tailed Tropic-bird (15)** may be the first to put in an appearance; the **White-tailed Tropic-bird (15)** is now seen also well out at sea. Between 150°W. and Hawaii considerable numbers of **White-necked Petrels (11)**, migrating from the Kermadec Is., and **Black-winged Petrels (12)** from New Zealand have been recorded between May and October. The Hawaiian and White-necked Petrels may easily be confused, their distinctive differences being described under the Hawaiian Petrel.

The Hawaiian islands

A great variety of seabirds have been recorded in the vicinity of this mid-ocean group of islands through extensive observations carried out by the Smithsonian Institution and other interested American ornithological societies. Many species have only been seen on rare occasions and are possibly only vagrants. The observer must be content in this narrative to consider only those most likely to be seen, and which breed within the group, together with other species which have been recorded on the shipping route.

The following list of breeding species may serve as a guide: **Laysan Albatross (4)**, **Black-footed Albatross (6)**, **Wedge-tailed** and **Christmas Shearwaters (7)**, **Newell's Shearwater, Bonin** and **Hawaiian Petrels (12)**, **Bulwer's Petrel (9)**, **Tristram's Storm-petrel (14)**, **Madeiran Storm-petrel (13)**, **White-tailed** and **Red-tailed Tropic-birds (15)**, **Brown** and **Red-footed Boobies (19)**, **Blue-faced Booby (18)**, **Great Frigate-bird (24)**, **Sooty** and **Spectacled Terns (44)**, **Common, Blue-grey** and **White-capped Noddies (44)** and **White Tern (43)**.

The breeding season of almost all these species covers an extended period and the birds are not free from nesting duties until the beginning of the autumn. More are likely to be seen at sea in the later months of the year.

The noddies, the White Tern, the Spectacled Tern and the Christmas Shearwater, which do not range so far to seaward from the islands, are unlikely to be seen although the Red-footed and Blue-faced Boobies have been reported occasionally. There are regular reports however from ships passing the islands of both Black-footed and Laysan Albatrosses, Wedge-tailed Shearwaters, Hawaiian and **Bulwer's Petrels (9)**, White-tailed and Red-tailed Tropic-birds, and Sooty Rerns.

ALBATROSSES. Both the Black-footed and Laysan Albatrosses breed in large numbers on the leeward Hawaiian chain and on conclusion of the breeding season tend to spread northwards ranging largely between 30°N. and 45°N. While both

Laysan Albatross

albatrosses certainly occur across the whole breadth of the N. Pacific, the Laysan Albatross is seen rather less frequently close to the Pacific coastline of N. America. Both species are constant ship followers, the Black-footed Albatross the bolder, the Laysan hanging back further astern. They will be the ship's principal companions, the greatest numbers probably during September and October.

The rare **Short-tailed Albatross (3)** would be a prize indeed if observed during the latter part of the voyage. At one time almost exterminated by feather hunters, a small group has re-established itself on Torishima I. in the Izu Is. south of Japan. It has only been reported once in the western quarter of the route by British ships.

Mid-Pacific area. Trans-Pacific migrants

The flyways of those shearwaters which undertake enormous migratory circuits between their southern ocean breeding stations and the N. Pacific outside the breeding seasons are still imperfectly known. The paths of certain Sooty Shearwaters and Pink-footed Shearwaters on the eastern side of the Pacific have been referred to in Route 20. But we have little information as to the precise routes adopted by the **Short-tailed Shearwaters (8)** which breed principally in Tasmania, the **Sooty** and **Grey-backed Shearwaters (8)** and **Peale's Petrel (12)** which breed in New Zealand, and the **Pale-footed Shearwater (8)** which breeds in Australia and New Zealand. All these species migrate into the N. Pacific and may be seen along the route more probably when flocks are on migration approximately between May and June and again between September and early November.

In addition it seems clear that certain petrels of the 'Cookilaria' group moving northward in winter months may reach the route.

Two examples from ships' observations throw some light on these movements. The first is from a west/east passage further south along the Equatorial Counter Current around latitude 7°N.: "On 3rd November between 176°W. and 173°W. Short-tailed Shearwaters came thick and fast, flying high for a shearwater at six to thirty feet, and with great speed, about 40 to 50 knots, zigzagging on a course between 190° and 200°. Flocks of up to 50 crossed our bows every 5 to 6 minutes and I calculated that during daylight we saw up to 400,000 birds. The next day between 168°W. and 166°W. birds were passing in flocks of up to 40. At this rate a million birds might pass through the funnel at 175°W. or perhaps two million over the whole area between 178°W. and 166°W. while the passage lasts." Grey-backed Shearwaters and Pale-footed Shearwaters in small numbers were also seen flying south in the same area.

Another observer during a northerly route from Japan to Texas has sighted flocks of Sooty Shearwaters between 40°N., 160°E. and 43°N., 175°E. from 17th to 19th August during three days, where separate flocks of between 100 and 200 birds were seen daily moving southwards.

From these examples a voyager in a ship on the route to Japan may be fortunate to add further information on these fascinating migration problems.

Midway Island to Japan

Passing Midway I. and during the entire latter part of the passage the ship will be accompanied daily by Black-footed and Laysan Albatrosses. At the outset Sooty Terns, Wedge-tailed Shearwaters and tropic-birds may occur, and a lookout should

Bonin Petrel

be kept for the **Bonin Petrel (12)** which breeds both on the western Hawaiian chain and the Bonin Is. south of Japan, and occurs regularly on the route at all seasons. Approximately halfway between Midway I. and Japan the first **White-faced Shearwater (8)** may be expected. This shearwater breeds on islands off the east coast of Japan and Taiwan and is abundant near its breeding quarters on the Izu Is. south of Yokohama during the breeding season in June and July. It spreads eastward during the non-breeding season and is abundant south of Japan in the China Sea, to the Philippines and other islands in the autumn and winter.

STORM-PETRELS. Both the Madeiran Storm-petrel and **Tristram's Storm-petrel (14)** breed on the leeward Hawaiian chain, the Madeiran Storm-petrel certainly also on Hide I. off Japan, but is rarely observed at sea. The Tristram's Storm-petrel is one of the largest storm-petrels, overall sooty-brown in plumage with a deeply forked tail, and the only all dark storm-petrel to be seen well to the east of Japan.

West of 160°E. an increase in the number and variety of seabirds may be expected. It is in this western sector that sightings of Peale's Petrel and Cook's Petrel have been reported in northern summer months, but more confirmation of their presence is certainly necessary. Wedge-tailed and White-faced Shearwaters and Bonin Petrels will continue to be seen, the Hawaiian Petrel, Sooty Tern and tropic-birds will have been left behind.

In the winter months the **Common Kittiwake (33, 39)** moves southward from the far N. Pacific to the area eastward of Japan and has been observed quite frequently on the route.

Coasts and harbours in Japan

The list of seabirds in 'Birds of Japan' (Yamashina) quotes no less than 72 species, 45 of which can be classed as vagrants. Even the most alert seafaring birdwatcher visiting ports in Honshu will never see many of these birds. One critical observer who has made many calls at ports has recorded only 18 species, and ships proceeding direct to and from main ports may see only those commonly resident.

In and around harbours the gulls most commonly seen may be listed as follows: **Japanese** and **Slaty-backed Gulls (27, 34)**, resident throughout the year; **Common** and **Herring Gulls (28, 35, 40)**, including the yellow-legged form of the latter; **Northern Black-headed Gull (28, 31, 32, 37, 40)**, frequent in winter and early spring. The **Little Tern (43)** and **Roseate Tern (42)** occur as summer visitors.

Both the **Common Cormorant (20, 23)** and the **Japanese Cormorant (20)** may be seen in the harbours. These birds are trained by fishermen to capture fish, the birds swimming around the fishing boats, collars fitted around their necks attached to long handling lines held by the fishermen.

In the north island of Hokkaido a number of different species of auks occur offshore but are uncommon further south. Both the **Spectacled Guillemot (46)** and **Crested Murrelet (48)** are resident locally.

MIGRANT SHEARWATERS, PHALAROPES AND SKUAS. Short-tailed Shearwaters and Pale-footed Shearwaters appear to the eastward of Japan in summer months during their migratory sweep into the N. Pacific. The possibility may arise of sighting **Pomarine** and **Arctic Skuas (26)** and the little **Red-necked Phalaropes (25)** on migration.

New Zealand to the Gulf of Panama

The sea route passes from southern temperate latitudes eastward and northward over cool surface waters until approximately 125°W., 30°S., thence onwards through warm surface waters of the tropical belt, later south of the Galapagos Is. meeting cool waters from the effect of the tail end of the northward flowing Humboldt Current, and finally reaching its destination in the heat of Balboa harbour.

The seabirds to be met with on the passage are governed by a number of factors. Certain species, for example those albatrosses local to the southern oceans, the Giant Petrel, the southern Great Skua, diving-petrels, prions, penguins, the latter local to the New Zealand coast, and many other shearwaters and petrels range over the cooler waters in the higher southern latitudes and are likely to disappear progressively as the passage proceeds. Others are found further north over warmer surface waters, while Sooty, Short-tailed, Pale-footed, Pink-footed Peale's or Mottled and Grey-backed Shearwaters undertake immense seasonal migrations during the southern autumn and winter months, crossing the Equator and reaching the higher latitudes of the N. Pacific, returning to their breeding quarters in the southern ocean in the southern spring and summer. Some petrels, such as the White-necked, Black-winged, Parkinson's, and Cook's Petrels also disperse through equatorial waters during their contra-nuptial seasons.

Vast numbers of tropical seabirds breed on islands in Oceania, some ranging further to seaward than others. During the voyage it will be only on passing the nearest points to Pitcairn and Ducie Is., and later on nearing the Galapagos Is. that the tropical boobies, terns, noddies, frigate-birds and tropic-birds are at all likely to be seen.

In this vast open ocean where seabirds cover great distances and their range is not fully known, it is only possible to define approximately where each species is perhaps most likely to be seen. Very many species inhabit the S. Pacific and have been observed at one time or another in the course of a number of passages. On a single voyage many will not be seen and often the ocean will appear an empty waste without a seabird in sight.

The route has been divided into separate sections covering the different seasons of the year.

All seasons – New Zealand to Pitcairn Island

The **Wandering Albatross (3)** is always most in evidence and has been recorded to within 1,000 miles south-west of Pitcairn I. **Black-browed Albatrosses (5)** may be seen to between 4 or 5 days steaming from New Zealand, the **Grey-headed Albatross (5)**, **Shy Albatross (4)** and **Light-mantled Sooty Albatross (6)** within the first three days to 160°W. approximately. The **Royal Albatross (3)** and **Buller's Albatross (4)** range much closer to New Zealand. The **Giant Petrel (6, 7)**, **Grey-faced Petrel (10)**, and southern **Great Skua (26)** may also be seen for the first three days.

At the outset of the voyage **Common Diving-petrels (14)**, **Fluttering Shearwaters**

Buller's Albatross

(10), Little Shearwaters (9), prions (11), White-faced, Black-bellied and **White-bellied Storm-petrels (13)** and **Grey-backed Storm-petrels (14)** may all be seen as well as Buller's, Bounty Island and Chatham Island Albatrosses.

'COOKILARIA' GROUP OF PETRELS. The 'Cookilaria' group of petrels occur throughout this section of the passage. Many petrels in the Pacific Ocean are very similar in size, plumage and characteristics. Particularly is this so in the case of certain 'Gadfly Petrels' of the genus *Pterodroma*: **Cook's, Stejneger's, Black-winged, Gould's Petrels (12)** and **Collared Petrels (12)**. The **Bonin Petrel (12)** is somewhat darker than the Black-winged Petrel, and is found only in the N. Pacific. The **Chatham Island Petrel** (p. 40) ranges over cool water east of New Zealand and is

Black-winged Petrel

unlikely to be seen on the present sea route. The first three species may be seen over this section of the route, moving more northward over warmer water and across the Equator during the southern winter.

All seasons – approaching Pitcairn Island

SHEARWATERS AND PETRELS. A distance of between 1,000 and 500 miles south-west of Pitcairn marks the usual limit of the sub-antarctic seabirds which range over cooler surface waters. The 'Cookilaria' group of petrels may still be seen as the passage approaches the warmer surface waters of the sub-tropical and tropical belts.

A lookout should be kept for the **Wedge-tailed Shearwater (7)**, which may now occur in both its dark and pale phases, and the **Christmas Shearwater (7)**, which has only been seen rarely on the sea route, and is believed to remain closer to the islands unlike the wide-ranging Wedge-tailed Shearwater. The Christmas Shearwater might be confused with the dark phase of the Wedge-tailed Shearwater, but is smaller in size, more chestnut in overall colour with a long dark slender bill and a wedge-shaped tail only half the length of the very noticeably long wedge tail of the shearwater bearing the name. Christmas Shearwaters breed at the nearest points to the route on Ducie, the Tuamotu and the Austral Is.

As the ship approaches Pitcairn I. a new group of petrels may be seen – the **Herald Petrel (10)**, the **Phoenix**, **Kermadec** and **Murphy's Petrels (12)**, all of which also breed on the Austral, Tuamotu and Henderson Is.

The Kermadec and Herald Petrels are very similar in appearance, the Kermadec distinctly larger however, lightly built with black-brown upperparts, long narrow wings and, particularly confusing, each may occur in both dark and pale phases with either brown or mottled brownish-white heads and brown or brown to almost white underparts. A quick clue is found by observing the underwing. The Kermadec Petrel shows a white circular patch near the outer part of its brown underwing; the Herald Petrel shows a narrow white lining to the underwing and no white patch. Both birds which breed nearer the Equator are said to be more usually in the dark phase. In the Phoenix Petrel the underbody is white except for a dark breast band and the underwings all dark. Murphy's Petrel appears as an overall brownish-black bird at sea.

Phoenix Petrels

OTHER SEABIRDS. **Sooty Terns (44)** and **Red-tailed Tropic-birds (15)** have been seen occasionally far out at sea in the area but it is most unlikely that frigate-birds, boobies or noddies will be seen so far from land.

Southern spring (October, November, December) – New Zealand to Pitcairn Island

In addition to those seabirds likely to be seen at all seasons, other species become increasingly evident.

During late October and November the New Zealand migrant shearwaters, the **Sooty, Pale-footed** and **Grey-backed Shearwaters (8)** are returning to their breeding areas in New Zealand. In addition the **White-chinned Petrel (7)**, **Brown Petrel (10)** and **White-headed** and **Pintado Petrels (11)** will occur, the latter often following ships as far as Pitcairn I.

The Sooty Shearwater is the 'Mutton Bird' of New Zealand. Larger but otherwise liable to be confused with the Short-tailed Shearwater, its underwing-coverts are much paler, almost silvery, compared with the greyish underwing-coverts of the Short-tailed species. The Pale-footed Shearwater is much larger and more heavily built, chocolate-black in colour with a very noticeable fleshy-white bill. The White-chinned Petrel should not be confused with the somewhat similar sized Pale-footed Shearwater, for although also chocolate-black in colour with a massive pale bill, it is a persistent ship follower, but in this area its white chin may be absent or hardly observable. Both the Brown Petrel and Pintado Petrel are regular ship followers, the 'piebald' Pintado Petrel being most distinctively patterned. The large heavily built Brown Petrel, brownish-grey in general colour with a long greenish-white bill, may be distinguished by its white underbody.

Indeed during the first three days of the voyage during the spring a great host of seabirds may be following, albatrosses, Giant Petrels, and flocks of prions and individual storm-petrels in addition to the above.

Southern summer (January, February, March) – New Zealand to Pitcairn Island

No mention has been made of the penguins which breed in New Zealand for they are rarely seen by ships. However on passing through the Cook Strait it is possible that they may be sighted. These short-necked stout-bodied birds swim very low in the water, exposing only head and neck, and are thus difficult to distinguish at sea by species. Being flightless they may sometimes be seen leaping and diving in an effort to escape the ship. Five species breed in New Zealand, the **Fiordland Crested, Yellow-eyed, Little or Blue, White-flippered** and **Erect-crested Penguins (2)**.

During the southern summer breeding season immature and non-breeding albatrosses will still be seen at sea in lesser numbers. The Wandering Albatross still ranges to within 1,000 miles of Pitcairn I., but other albatrosses may well be absent after the third day out on the voyage. Large numbers of 'Cookilaria' petrels may be expected at the outset, and prions, which complete their breeding season somewhat earlier, increase in numbers by March.

The three New Zealand migrant shearwaters will still be met with within a few hundred miles of New Zealand. Other 'all season' species may of course be seen.

Southern autumn (April, May, June) – New Zealand to Pitcairn Island

The New Zealand migrant shearwaters are likely to have left the area by late May for northern latitudes. The sighting of albatrosses remains unchanged, and other sub-antarctic breeding species tend to increase during the latter half of the autumn. White-chinned and White-headed Petrels should be seen during the first three or four days of the voyage, while Grey-faced Petrels have been seen to within 1,000 miles of Pitcairn I. and a number of 'Cookilaria' petrels as far as Pitcairn itself. Other 'all season' species will be in the area.

Southern winter (July, August, September) – New Zealand to Pitcairn Island

The absence of the migrant shearwaters is offset by a movement into more temperate waters of sub-antarctic species. Several dozen Wandering Albatrosses have been known to follow a ship at the outset and they have been recorded 500 miles south-west of Pitcairn. Black-browed, Grey-headed and Light-mantled Sooty Albatrosses and perhaps one or two Royal Albatrosses are likely to be seen. Giant Petrels are numerous, following a ship for several days, and the southern Great Skua in addition. Brown Petrels and Pintado Petrels are constant ship followers, and the Grey-faced Petrel is numerous for several hundred miles from New Zealand. The White-chinned Petrel and the White-headed Petrel are more frequent, and on occasions flocks of 'Cookilaria' petrels are seen. Storm-petrels may be seen as far as Pitcairn. The **Erect-crested Penguin (2)** occurs off Cook Strait in winter.

All seasons – Pitcairn Island to Galapagos Islands

The seabirds which may be seen on approaching Pitcairn have already been mentioned. A rare species, **Parkinson's Petrel (7)**, might possibly be seen; it is very similar indeed in aspect but smaller than the White-chinned Petrel but does not show a white chin and is not known to follow ships.

In the wide stretch of the tropical Pacific north-east of Pitcairn, few seabirds have been reported; sightings are likely to be very much a matter of chance encounter between long intervals. Grey-backed Shearwaters have been observed in March and June, and again south-west of Pitcairn in November indicating a migrating route, Cook's Petrels spread similarly in March and November.

As the ship approaches the meridian of 105°W. seabirds become more frequent. A lookout should be kept for the **Hawaiian Petrel (12)**, and as the ship nears the Galapagos Is. **Audubon's Shearwater (9)**.

Certain Shearwaters and petrels which move northwards over warmer waters during the southern winter, but whose oceanic distribution is by no means fully known, notably Cook's, Stejneger's and Kermadec Petrels have been seen between June and October. Sooty Shearwaters and **Pink-footed Shearwaters (8)**, which breed during the southern summer off the coast of Chile, migrate far north to the coasts of Alaska during the southern winter, and these may also be passing through the area, more probably during May to July and October and November. Certainly the majority of records of these two shearwaters have occurred south-east of the Galapagos Is., very large 'rafts' of Sooty Shearwaters and numbers of Pink-footed Shearwaters having been seen in June and August. **White-necked Petrels (11)**, which breed in the Juan Fernandez Is. off the Chilean coast between December and June, are most likely to be seen on the route between May and October, but usually only singly.

The Pink-footed Shearwater can be distinguished most easily from the Pale-footed Shearwater by its white underparts and whitish underwings. The White-necked Petrel and Hawaiian Petrel, gadfly petrels with a distinctive swooping and soaring flight, can easily be confused. The later, however, is much darker above.

All seasons – approaching the Galapagos Islands

As the ship nears the Galapagos Is. it will be passing through cool surface water arising from the tail end of the northward flowing cold Humboldt Current. The Galapagos Is. provide a breeding area largely between May and August for a variety of tropical seabirds, not all of which will be seen from a ship on the direct route to Panama, but which nevertheless are worthy of record. On these unique islands may be found nesting the **Waved Albatross (4)**, Audubon's Shearwater, Hawaiian Petrel, **Elliot's Storm-petrel (13)**, **Red-billed Tropic-bird (15)**, **Blue-faced Booby (18)**, **Blue-footed** and **Red-footed Boobies (19)**, **Great Frigate-bird (24)**, **Common Noddy (44)**, **Galapagos** and **Madeiran Storm-petrels (13)**, **Swallow-tailed Gull (33, 39)**, **Dusky Gull (30, 33, 38)**, **Flightless Cormorant (20)** and **Galapagos Penguin (1)**. Amongst this wealth of birds, any of which with the exception of the cormorant and penguin are likely to be seen on the route from now onwards, a special lookout should be kept for the Waved Albatross, the only albatross confined to the tropics and local to the eastern quarter of the Pacific. Its size and typical 'albatross flight' should distinguish it from any other seabird in the area.

In this area too may be seen a variety of storm-petrels, to be mentioned later, of which however the Galapagos Storm-petrel predominates.

Galapagos Islands to Panama Bay

The seabirds local to the Gulf of Panama are described later, and the occurrence of Sooty Shearwaters and Pink-footed Shearwaters has already been referred to, but the area off Ecuador and Peru is a favourite wintering area at sea for phalaropes. These dainty little waders breed in the far northern hemisphere, spending the autumn and winter months in the open sea in certain favourite areas in warm climates where upwelling water provides abundant plankton.

Here the **Red-necked** and **Grey Phalaropes (25)** congregate, while the less common **Wilson's Phalarope (25)** passes through the area to winter generally further south off the coast of S. America. These small long-necked waders usually collect in flocks, parties resting on the water or taking short flights not unlike sandpipers. Between late autumn and early spring they may be seen on the route, at these seasons in winter plumage.

STORM-PETRELS ALONG THE ROUTE. Storm-petrels range widely over the Pacific Ocean and may appear spasmodically. Suddenly one or two mainly dark little seabirds will be seen crisscrossing the wake, fluttering and dipping their legs to the surface, or perhaps flying with greater freedom and taking no notice of the ship. Their very small size will classify them as storm-petrels but positive identification of species at sea is always difficult. At the outset of the voyage the White-faced Storm-petrel, the White-bellied and Black-bellied species and the Grey-backed Storm-petrel have already been mentioned.

Wilson's Storm-petrel (13) migrates northwards during the southern winter within the Humboldt Current and may be seen during May/June and October/November. Other species which occur in the area between the Galapagos Is. and the Gulf of Panama are the Galapagos, Madeiran and Elliot's Storm-petrels, which breed on the islands, the Pacific race of **Leach's Storm-petrel (13)**, the **Black** and **Least Storm-petrels (14)**, the smallest of all the storm-petrels. **Hornby's Storm-petrel (14)** has been reported but its range is more southerly off the west coast of S. America.

PASSERS-BY. There remain certain globe-spanning migrants which breed in the northern hemisphere and escape the northern winter by immense migrations deep into the southern hemisphere, and may pass across the route between the Galapagos and the Gulf of Panama. The **Pomarine Skua (26)** has been seen on more than one occasion in the autumn en route for the west coast of S. America, and the **Arctic Skua (26)** does likewise. The **Arctic Tern (41, 42)** has also been reported, but the problem of tern identification at sea is so difficult that its presence has yet to be confirmed from further reports from sea.

The reader who has covered this route once only may be confused and disappointed at the total of his 'record of species', for the narrative is based upon the total of many voyages added together. At the outset and termination of his voyage his log is likely to fill generously, but during the long days of mid-ocean travel extensive gaps are likely to occur. There will be other compensations: shoals of alarmed flying fish, the blowing of whales, and the many spectacular meteorological effects which a voyager in this wide ocean may be privileged to witness.

The Panama Canal and Gulf of Panama

The Gulf of Panama is a focal area common to ships passing through the Canal from both the Atlantic and Pacific Oceans. Some of the seabirds mentioned will have already been seen by these ships, but others may be new, and an account of the great variety which occur in this area will provide either a beginning or an end to a long ocean voyage. The birds quoted within the Gulf of Panama extend broadly between the anchorage and 100°W.

THE PANAMA CANAL. The Canal, one of the greatest engineering feats of its time, blasted and carved through wet tropical mosquito infested jungle, must cause every traveller today passing through the Gatun Lock, the great Culebra Cut and so onward through the Miraflores Locks, to look entranced at the beauty and variety of the scenery on either side.

Quite a number of seabirds populate the waters of the Canal, amongst those most frequently seen being **Brown Pelicans (17)**, both **Bigua** and **Double-crested Cormorants (21)**, often seen perched on buoys, **Magnificent Frigate-birds (24)**, usually circling overhead, **Laughing Gulls (31, 36)** around the locks, the occasional **Royal Tern (41)** and more frequently in the autumn and winter **Common Gulls (28, 35, 40)** and **Black Terns (44)**, sometimes reported in flocks. Occasionally an **American White Pelican (17)** has been seen at the eastern entrance to the Canal.

THE GULF OF PANAMA. Close to the anchorage the birds mentioned throughout the Canal transit are equally common. A close inspection of the frigate-birds may result however in **Great Frigate-birds (24)** being among them. Further to the west this species certainly replaces the Magnificent Frigate-bird. **Little Terns (43)** occur in the anchorage at all seasons and both **Brown Boobies (19)** and **Blue-faced Boobies**

(18). Between autumn and the spring a lookout should be kept for three gulls which winter in the area, **Franklin's Gull (30, 31, 36)**, **Bonaparte's Gull (31, 36)** and **Sabine's Gull (33, 39)**. The first are reported rarely, but the distinctively plumaged Sabine's Gull may be seen sometimes as late as May from the coast of Colombia southwards.

Further out into the Gulf two further species of the booby family, the **Red-footed** and **Blue-footed Boobies (19)**, and **Red-billed Tropic-birds (15)** may be seen for the first time.

Panama to Valparaiso – Coastwise

The seabirds to be seen in the Gulf of Panama are described in Route 20. The route now described continues southwards past Ecuador and beyond.

Nowhere at sea in the world will such large concentrations of seabirds be seen daily, sometimes in enormous numbers, as when a voyager is undertaking a coastwise passage down the west coast of S. America, the 'Guanay Coast'. The cold Humboldt Current sweeps northwards supplying an abundance of surface feed in which anchovies play a leading part. For centuries millions of seabirds have thrived and multiplied along the whole length of the coastline. It is only when steaming from port to port at no great distance from the coast that a ship will pass through the seaward range of the great majority of the birds; eighty miles to seaward and beyond there will be little chance of seeing the pelicans, boobies, cormorants, gulls and terns, the chief actors in this pageant of seabirds.

Unlike other sea passages where the appearance of different species may be anticipated progressively, in this case they share the honours in many cases at all points down the coast at all seasons. There are oceanic species and a few others which undertake long winter and summer migrations which occur only at certain seasons.

The route, omitting calls at ports, presupposes the average longitude as between the coast and 80°W. off mid-Peru at 10°S., becoming 75°W. at 16°S., and thence 71°W. to Valparaiso. Such vast numbers are involved that the description which follows is intended to give but one example of typical 'daily counts' of species taken

Inca Tern

Chilean Pelican preparing to dive

during a single passage with passing reference to the seabird life in harbours. It is less a progress, but rather a pattern of the enormous numbers of birds seen.

Pelicans and cormorants are most active at dawn and dusk diving in perpetual streams close around ships, a spectacle aptly described as 'raining birds'. This continues after dark in the glow of ships' lights. At other times the 'Guanay Birds' together with gulls and Inca Terns fly into harbours as the sun sets to commence their evening feed, all but a handful dispersing to sea during the day.

Southward bound in summer months

Perhaps one of the features along the coast apart from the resident coastal seabirds is the far northward penetration of certain southern ocean shearwaters and petrels, excluding truly migratory species, which move northward within the Humboldt Current during the southern winter. In July the **Pintado Petrel (11)**, **Southern Fulmar (11)**, and **White-chinned Petrel (7)** have been observed at 8.5°S. No doubt but a few reach this latitude.

At any point along the coast of Ecuador to perhaps 12°S., occasional sightings of the **Waved Albatross (4)**, and other seabirds seen in the Gulf of Panama, may occur. The albatross breeds on the Galapagos Is. and is the only albatross confined entirely to the tropics, its range being limited to the cool adjacent surface waters. This large albatross with its greyish-brown back, upperwings and tail, white head, buffish-grey nape and dusky-white underparts cannot be confused with any other seabirds in the area.

From now onwards throughout the passage to Valparaiso great flocks of up to 500 **Chilean Pelicans (17)** and similar numbers of **Peruvian Boobies (19)** and **Guanay Cormorants (22)** may be counted daily. **Red-legged** and **Bigua Cormorants (21)** tend to range closer inshore into bays and harbours.

Daily counts of **Grey Gulls (30, 38)** and **Southern Black-backed Gulls (27, 34, 40)** following the ship may run into hundreds. **Simeon Gulls (30, 34, 38)** are usually in smaller numbers, the highest daily count of 150 occurring at Matarani, Peru, after which they tend to disappear south of the N. Chilean coast. **Inca Terns (44)** and **Chilean Terns (43)** are also seen daily in small numbers from central Peru to Valparaiso.

In addition two other gulls, the **Grey-headed Gull (30, 36, 38)** and **Andean Gull (30, 36)** have been recorded and the **Patagonian Black-headed Gull (31, 36)** in ports in southern Chile.

In addition to this pattern of daily sightings, other truly oceanic species come into the picture.

ALBATROSSES, SHEARWATERS and PETRELS. Reaching 10°S., slightly north of Callao in June the northward trend already mentioned can be amplified. There have been daily sightings of up to 4 or 5 **Shy Albatrosses (4)** and 20 immature **Giant Petrels (6, 7)** from 10°S. onward to 26°S. Pintado Petrels are likely to pick up a ship at perhaps 20°S. and will continue to Valparaiso. The first **Wandering Albatross (3)** may be seen at about 25°S., numbers increasing, mostly in immature plumage, to daily counts of up to 15 or more as far as Valparaiso at 33°S. Soon after the 'Wanderer', the first **Black-browed Albatross (5)** may be expected increasing to considerable numbers south of Valparaiso. White-chinned Petrels are likely to appear following a ship at about 25°S., to be joined by Southern Fulmars and an increased number of Pintado Petrels.

No mention has yet been made of the mass migration of **Sooty Shearwaters (8)** and to a lesser extent in numbers of the **Pink-footed Shearwaters (8)** northwards in the Humboldt Current which appears to reach its peak during June. Sooty Shearwaters breed inland from the sea coast of Chile and on islands off Cape Horn, Pink-footed Shearwaters in the Juan Fernandez Is. and on Mocha I.

During the southward sea passage in early summer the appearance of both species may well be noticed as far north as Ecuador. An account from one bird log illustrates what may be in store at this time. Sooty Shearwaters were first encountered at 5°S., off Ecuador on 3rd June, rafts increasing from 100 to 2,000 at 11°S., to an estimated 20,000 in separate large flocks at 16°S. on 18th June, visible on the ship's radar out to 10 miles. Large sightings continued as far as 25°S. after which only small parties were seen as far south as Talcahuano Bay, 37°S. Incidentally as many as 200 White-chinned Petrels were counted at 31°S. on 25th June.

The movements and numbers of Pink-footed Shearwaters are less well defined but it is clear that they start moving northwards somewhat earlier as they have been seen in large numbers north of Callao at 10°S. in mid-May.

OTHER PETRELS and STORM-PETRELS. The identification at sea of many very similar S. Pacific petrels of the 'gadfly' races is always a matter of difficulty. Reports of **Cook's** and **Stejneger's Petrels (12)** south of 25°S. have occurred but much more positive information is needed before the range of a number of species within the coastal limits of the Humboldt Current can be defined.

An unusual number of species of storm-petrels are to be seen along the length of the west coast of S. America. As usual they are very difficult to identify by species at sea and none can say where they may be most expected, with the possible exception of the Galapagos and Elliot's Storm-petrels. One example of this point may be given from the remarkable occurrence in one ship. Fish meal was loaded on board at Chimbote, 9°S. Was it the smell of the cargo which resulted in the arrival ON BOARD during the night of 24th July of a remarkable assortment of storm-petrels, discovered all over the decks the next morning? Here were 25

Wilson's Storm-petrels (13), 2 Elliot's Storm-petrels (13), 2 Hornby's Storm-petrels (14), 8 Galapagos Storm-petrels (13), one White-bellied Storm-petrel (13), and indeed two Pink-footed Shearwaters. All were fully measured, described in detail and photographed – a unique event. With the exception of the Galapagos and Elliot's Storm-petrels, the remaining species have been identified far further south at other seasons, and, while it is known that Wilson's and the White-bellied Storm-petrels undoubtedly move north of the Equator during the southern winter, it is difficult to give more than an indication where these may be seen along the route. The Wilson's Storm-petrel breeds on islands off Cape Horn, Hornby's breeds inland along the Chilean coast and the White-bellied on the Juan Fernandez Is., and these may be expected therefore well southwards. Elliot's and the Galapagos Storm-petrels breed on the Galapagos Is. and are certainly most likely to be seen off Ecuador. Here too another storm-petrel which has been recorded off Peru, the large fork-tailed **Markham's Storm-petrel (14)**, must be added to the list. They form a formidable problem in identification to any birdwatcher at sea.

Markham's Storm-petrel

OTHER SEABIRDS. The **Great Skua (26)** is something of an enigma. In May and June and again in October these have been noticed several times, usually singly, between 9° and 11°S. and these may be of the northern race. During the same months they have also occurred from 16° to 23°S. onwards, almost certainly southern Great Skuas. It is likely that they will be seen throughout the whole route at all times of the year. **Pomarine** and **Arctic Skuas (26)** evidently migrate northwards and southwards along the coast during the northern spring and autumn. Some Pomarine Skuas winter off Ecuador while Arctic Skuas have been seen as far south as Talcahuano, 37°S., during January.

Northern winter

There is little change in the numbers of the 'Guanay Birds', S. American gulls and terns, but two new species, the **Sabine's Gull (33, 39)** and **Franklin's Gull (30, 31, 36)** occur as winter migrants. Sabine's Gull breeds in the far north arctic regions and undertakes a long southerly migration, numbers beginning to appear in the Gulf of Panama southwards along the coast to Chile in September, increasing in numbers through the winter. A count has been recorded of 470 Sabine's Gulls at 14°S. and over 100 at 8°S. in February. Franklin's Gulls breed inland in N. America and spread further southwards down the coast being recorded as far as Coquimbo, 30°S., in January. They may be seen in April and May off Ecuador during their northward migration.

Outside the coastal zone

An indication of the dearth of seabirds outside the coastal zone may be quoted from a passage from a ship steering directly northwards from Talcahuana, 37°S., towards Ecuador in mid-July. The ship was 180 miles offshore at 30°S., increasing to 240 miles at 20°S. and only closing the coast midway up the coast of Peru. For this reason the usual flocks of pelicans, boobies, cormorants, gulls and terns were entirely absent. In the first two days a single Southern Fulmar, a few White-chinned Petrels and Pintado Petrels and one or two White-bellied Storm-petrels and other 'Cookilaria' petrels were seen. Only one Wandering Albatross was seen and no others until a Waved Albatross appeared at 4.5°S. Sooty and Pink-footed Shearwaters were entirely absent until close to the coast at 11°S. when 2,000 were recorded.

Seabirds in harbours – daily counts

The picture is very much the same in the many harbours in which daily counts have been taken and four ports spread down the coast illustrate the general pattern.

SAMANCO BAY, PERU, 9°S.   June
Approaching the bay, 100 Chilean Pelicans, 20 Peruvian Boobies, 200 Guanay Cormorants, 100 Inca Terns. Daily counts in harbour averaged up to 100 pelicans, 250 Red-legged Cormorants, 20 Peruvian Boobies, 30 Grey Gulls, a dozen Southern Black-backed Gulls, and an occasional Simeon Gull and Chilean Tern.

MATARANI, PERU, 17°S.   June
10 Humboldt Penguins, very large numbers of Chilean Pelicans, and Guanay Cormorants, 10 Red-legged Cormorants, 50 Grey Gulls, 50 Southern Black-backed Gulls, 150 Simeon Gulls, 10 Inca Terns, no Peruvian Boobies. About 2,000 Chilean Pelicans colonising Pinta Islay Is., and Red-legged Cormorants and Inca Terns observed nesting in September.

IQUIQUE, CHILE, 20°S.   June
200 Chilean Pelicans, 50 Guanay Cormorants, 2,000 Grey Gulls, 1,000 Southern Black-backed Gulls, 20 Inca Terns.

VALPARAISO, CHILE, 33°S.   July
15 Humboldt Penguins, 2,000 Chilean Pelicans, up to 500 Peruvian Boobies, 2,000 Guanay Cormorants, 25 Grey Gulls, 100 Patagonian Black-headed Gulls, few Red-legged Cormorants and Bigua Cormorants, 500 Southern Black-backed Gulls, and occasional Andean Gulls and Inca Terns.

Winter

In autumn and winter months the Sabine's Gulls and Black Terns appear in the northern ports and from one log there occur entries of an immense flock of 6,000 Black Terns and 200 Sabine Gulls at 5°S. in January, with 26 Sabine's Gulls at Matarani, while Franklin's Gulls are spreading into harbours further south.

ROUTE 22

Buenos Aires to Valparaiso via the Straits of Magellan

A passage from Buenos Aires to Valparaiso through the Straits of Magellan will take a ship further south than on any other shipping route and into the heart of the oceanic range of the seabirds of the southern oceans.

There is a general northward dispersion up both coasts of S. America on completion of the southern spring/summer breeding season by many seabirds which breed in the Falkland Is., the southern tip of S. America and in the sub-antarctic islands. During the passage many of the oceanic species will be seen at all seasons, but an increasing number range as far north as Buenos Aires and Valparaiso, and indeed well beyond, during the southern winter months from May onwards. Immature non-breeding birds often linger on into October and November while adults are returning to their southern breeding areas.

Detailed personal accounts of the seabirds to be met within the Straits of Magellan must be relatively rare.

Southwards from Buenos Aires towards Tierra del Fuego

At the outset during the passage past La Plata to the open sea the **Southern Black-backed Gull (27, 34, 40)** will be the commonest species likely to be following the ship, but **Patagonian Black-headed Gulls (31, 36)** may also be seen, and both species are recorded as following at some distance to seaward. The **Grey-headed Gull (30, 36, 38)** has been seen less frequently and has not been recorded offshore.

Grey-headed and Patagonian Black-headed Gulls

In winter the plumage of both the Patagonian Black-headed and the Grey-headed Gulls is very similar, but the latter shows darker grey underwing-coverts and sufficient grey remains on its head to distinguish it.

Magellan Penguins (1), which breed in the Falkland Is. and islands around Tierra del Fuego, disperse northwards and small groups may be seen by ships off the seaward entrance to the River Plate. They have been seen throughout the route towards the Falkland Is. 200 miles from the coast. Terns have also been observed occasionally, almost certainly **South American Terns (42)**.

OCEANIC SPECIES. Throughout the southward passage certain albatrosses and petrels will be seen at all seasons. **Wandering Albatrosses (3)** and **Black-browed Albatrosses (5)** will close and sail by the ship, planing steeply towards the sea downwind with wings bent at the wrist, banking and rising into the wind on the updraught from the waves, wings fully extended, and turning once again to sweep downward in an ever repeated cycle. Wandering Albatrosses are likely to put in an appearance more often. In the early part of the passage **Schlegel's Petrels (10)** are to be seen frequently. During the southern winter months in particular flocks of little **prions (11)** may be met with, flashing grey and white as they tilt and twist in rapid concerted flight. The dark inverted W pattern on their upperwings and the sight of a dark tipped white tail will identify these little 'Whale Birds' as they are called.

Pintado Petrels (11) with their unmistakable piebald plumage, **Giant Petrels (6, 7)**, these large greyish-brown 'Nellies' or 'Stinkers' as they are called by seamen, having none of the grace of an albatross, are regular ship followers, and **White-chinned Petrels (7)**, large, almost black and distinguished best by their large very pale bills, are also likely to be seen. The **Grey-headed Albatross (5)** breeds in the Falkland Is., Cape Horn, S. Georgia and elsewhere and has been recorded on several occasions, tending to range well to the south. At sea in the changing conditions of light the similarity of adults with adult Yellow-nosed Albatrosses is a constant cause for confusion. The colour of their mantles and upperwing-surfaces is very similar and both have mainly black bills showing a yellow edge. To claim the adult Grey-headed Albatross one must look for a noticeably grey head and neck, the appearance of a white crescent behind the eye and a critical look at the bill. This shows a yellow stripe along the middle of the upper mandible with a pink tip, and an

Grey-headed Albatross

additional yellow band along the base of the lower mandible. Furthermore it is particularly difficult in certain stages of immature plumage in the Grey-headed Albatross to distinguish between it and the similar immature Black-browed Albatross. In the Grey-headed the whole head and neck looks brownish-grey where it meets and is sharply divided from the white on throat and breast, quite distinct from the manner in which the grey blends gradually into the white in the young Black-browed Albatross.

Late southern spring

Observations along this part of the route bounded to the east by the S. Atlantic indicate that a variety of oceanic species which may well have been wintering further north are returning towards their southerly breeding areas. From October through to December **Great Shearwaters (9)** have been seen along the route between 37° and 45°S. flying eastwards, and **Sooty Shearwaters (8)**, **Wilson's Storm-petrels (13)**, sometimes in considerable flocks, and occasional **White-bellied Storm-petrels (13)** will be seen.

As the ship approaches the latitude of the Falkland Is. both **Rock-hopper Penguins (2)** and **Magellan Penguins**, which have been observed at sea 200 miles north of the islands, could occur on the route and a lookout should be kept for southern **Great Skuas (26)** and an occasional **Southern Fulmar (11)**.

The Straits of Magellan

As one approaches the Straits of Magellan from the Atlantic one's first impression is one of rather uninteresting low-lying land to the north. To the south lies Terra del Fuego "the land of fire", the mountainous and tree-covered aspect of which Charles Darwin wrote "It is doubtful if a single acre of flat land exists in such an area". Many columns of smoke support this derivation, for at night the clouds reflect the reddened glow and one is reminded of tropical storms.

The voyage through the Straits consists of two distinct phases, the open water to Punta Arenas, followed by a tenuous route through many alternative narrow passages leading to the open ocean. Invariably strong westerly winds carry a warning from the snow-covered mountains that lie ahead.

Southern Black-backed Gulls will follow the ship in company with Giant Petrels, White-chinned Petrels and southern Great Skuas. Along the low kelp-covered mud flats **South American Terns (42)** will be feeding, but it is not until the ship anchors off Punta Arenas that the greatest variety of bird life will be seen. Here Wilson's Storm-petrels flutter and dance astern of the ship, Giant Petrels float buoyantly amongst a flock of Southern Black-backed Gulls, southern Great Skuas swoop and harry the gulls and long undulating lines of **Magellan Cormorants (22)** can be seen flying between their nesting and feeding grounds well clear of the port area. The inshore waters of the Straits are full of thick kelp; Magellan Penguins venture to within a few miles of the port and Elephant Seals surface and bask amongst the kelp.

Leaving Punta Arenas the Cordilleras lie close ahead shrouded in cloud, and as the channel narrows one gains the impression of being landlocked within a dark green box with the ugly grey sky forming the lid. The mountains fall sheer, small pockets of mist rolling endlessly along their slopes where gnarled trees fight a constant battle to gain a foothold, their precarious attitudes bearing witness of the gales in these extreme climatic conditions.

In March the scene is somewhat altered by the summer thaw, but much snow remains on the mountains, many glaciers exist and continue to shed falls of ice into the green waters. Numerous narrow waterfalls appear as icicles hanging from the clouds. Bird life becomes more profuse; besides the ever-present gulls, White-chinned and Giant Petrels, fleeting glimpses of **Magellan Diving-petrels (14)** occur. Of all the birds however, the Black-browed Albatrosses claim precedence. In one particular area comprising a maze of small thickly wooded islands Black-browed Albatrosses can be seen on all sides and a breeding area must exist. Groups of Magellan Cormorants may be seen fishing between the many islands while the southern Great Skua favours the kelp patches.

Human life is scarce and wildlife enjoys an undisturbed natural environment. One or two groups of Indians may be seen, their presence betrayed by dugout canoes and wisps of smoke emerging from amongst the trees. Fish are abundant, the channels sometimes teeming with rising fish, and Killer Whales are not infrequent visitors. All too soon if the weather be kind, but none too soon if a force 9 gale is in the offing, will the ship sight the Pacific Ocean ahead.

The route north

On emerging from the Straits of Magellan it is only when a ship steams northwards coastwise at no great distance from the land that the full numbers of seabirds will be appreciated. The southern coast of Chile is bordered by innumerable islands many of which must surely provide breeding areas, hitherto undetected, for seabirds.

Gulls and Guanay birds collect around fishing boats and many of the oceanic petrels, storm-petrels and albatrosses have been observed within 20 miles of the land. This has already been referred to in Route 21, covering observations both in the southern winter and southern summer periods.

The present route northwards covers a period from the end of March onwards when a northward dispersion is already beginning. Wandering and Black-browed Albatrosses and Giant Petrels will pick up and follow the ship again, White-chinned Petrels will be seen crossing the wake and Grey-headed Albatrosses, southern Great Skuas, Southern Fulmars, Pintado Petrels and prions may all be seen.

At the end of March considerable flocks of **Sooty Shearwaters (8)** have been seen at 50°S. flying northwards, and at 22 miles west of the Chiloe Is., to quote one log, "Huge flocks of Sooty Shearwaters are everywhere flying northwards over large areas of drifting kelp". On the same day, 25th March, "The ship suddenly entered an area with a tremendous number of Wilson's Storm-petrels to be seen at all points of the compass and all flying northwards very close to the sea. This migration continued for over 4 hours as the ship steamed at 16 knots with the birds in sight as far as the eye could see."

From further north off Mocha I. on 26th March comes one report: "The sight to greet the eyes was truly amazing. As far as one could see huge flocks of Sooty Shearwaters and **Pink-footed Shearwaters (8)** were all heading for the sea flying north-northwest. Pink-footed Shearwaters breed on Mocha I. and Juan Fernandez Is. and in this case were doubtless moving to seaward for the day's feeding." These rather large shearwaters with greyish-brown upperparts, white underparts and underwing-coverts, and long yellow bills cannot easily be confused with other species along the coast.

OTHER SPECIES OF PETRELS AND STORM-PETRELS. 'Gadfly petrels' of the 'Cookilaria' group have been sighted off southern Chile from time to time but individual identification at sea is at all times difficult to establish. It seems probable that these infrequent observations were either **Cook's** or **Stejneger's Petrels (12)**, the latter breeding on Masafuera and Juan Fernandez Is.

Several species of storm-petrels range down the west coast of S. America. Both the very similar **Black-bellied** and **White-bellied Storm-petrels (13)**, **Hornby's** and **Markham's Storm-petrels (14)** may be seen.

Markham's Storm-petrel is distinctive in its large size, overall sooty-brown plumage, somewhat paler upperwing-coverts, black wing quills and deeply forked tail but its range is further north off Peru. Hornby's Storm-petrel is considerably smaller, with greyer upperparts, a white forehead and collar, and white underparts with a noticeable dark breast band. Its tail also is deeply forked. The rather smaller dark Black-bellied and White-bellied Storm-petrels both have white areas above the rump, white bellies and white underwing-coverts; the longitudinal dark band in the middle of the belly of the Black-bellied species is not always present or at least not noticeably present, and doubt as to correct identity when observed at sea is inevitable.

COASTAL GULLS AND TERNS. Once again the Southern Black-backed Gull is the commonest species, but as the ship continues northwards past Talcahuano **Grey Gulls (30, 38)** will become plentiful; at this stage Southern Black-backed and Grey Gulls will be following the ship. Closer inshore the Patagonian Black-headed Gull is sure to be seen and in the harbours the **Andean Gull (30, 36)** and **Franklin's Gull (30, 31, 36)** occur regularly. Although Franklin's Gull is a wintering visitor, breeding in central N. America, lingerers, as in the case of other migrant gulls, are to be seen throughout the year.

Terns are seen regularly in harbours, the handsome **Inca Tern (44)** being quite unmistakable. South American Terns which occur on both the east and west coasts are also likely to be present.

THE GUANAY BIRDS. The outstanding feature of the coastal seabird life of the west coast of S. America is the abundance of Guanay birds, the **Chilean Pelicans (17)**, **Peruvian Boobies (19)**, Guanay Cormorants (22), **Red-legged Cormorants (21)** and to a much lesser extent **Bigua Cormorants (21)** which feed in thousands both offshore and in the harbours, extending southwards to Valparaiso, and are seen at all seasons. They are mentioned in greater detail in Route 21.

The end of the voyage

Many different species have been mentioned but unlike any other long sea voyage perhaps the most unique feature will have been the almost constant companionship of albatrosses, White-chinned Petrels, Giant Petrels, southern Great Skuas, storm-petrels and other southern oceanic species. Occasionally Magellan and **Humboldt Penguins (1)** will have been seen.

As the ship approaches Valparaiso bay the first sighting is likely to be of Chilean Pelicans, Peruvian Boobies and Guanay Cormorants perched on the mooring buoys at Vina-del-Mar. Southern Black-backed Gulls, Grey Gulls and Andean Gulls will be flocking round any Guanay birds seen diving. Andean Gulls have a habit of perching on the backs of Chilean Pelicans as these birds surface after fishing, the gulls endeavouring to snatch some morsel as the pelican gulps down his fish. The inner harbour will be alive with gulls and terns around the fishing boats. Such is the variety and number of birds to be seen, particularly at dawn and dusk as the Guanay birds leave and return from sea that one cannot adequately describe the ever-changing conditions.

Gulf of Panama to Vancouver –
onward to the Bering Sea

The sea route northwards past the west coast of North America and Canada provides the observer with a great variety of seabirds ranging from tropical and sub-tropical species at the outset to oceanic species in the Gulf of Alaska, and the trans-equatorial migrants on passage. Should the ship call at such ports as San Francisco and Vancouver on the way, many species of inshore gulls are also likely to be seen.

The outset of the passage

Casting an eye around Balboa Roads, one is bound to notice the inevitable **Brown Pelicans (17)** and likely to catch sight of **Magnificent Frigate-birds (24)** circling overhead, as well as several **Brown Boobies (19)**. Less likely are the **Bigua Cormorant (21)** and possibly the **Double-crested Cormorant (21)**.

The **Laughing Gull (31, 36)** is common around the harbour and, of the terns, the **Royal Tern (41)**, **Common Tern (42, 43)**, **Little Tern (43)** and **Black Tern (44)** can all be anticipated, the latter having been seen frequently in the Gulf of Panama in the autumn.

Emerging into the Gulf of Panama, both **Sooty Terns (44)** and **Brown-winged Terns (44)** are likely to be seen, often making use of pieces of floating timber as perches. Here too one may see **Blue-faced Boobies (18)**, **Red-footed Boobies (19)** and the **Red-billed Tropic-bird (15)**.

Autumn, winter, early spring

At these seasons, three species of gulls, **Franklin's (30, 31, 36)**, **Bonaparte's (31, 36)** and **Sabine's (33, 39)**, winter locally and some may remain until May.

The northward passage

As the ship clears the Gulf and turns northwards towards the coasts of Mexico and Lower California at no great distance from the coast, many species already mentioned still occur. Brown and Blue-faced Boobies, Red-footed Boobies, Red-billed and Red-tailed Tropic-birds and, close inshore, Brown Pelicans, the latter as far north as San Francisco.

STORM-PETRELS. A lookout should be kept at this stage for the first sighting of the large **Black Storm-petrel (14)**. This large, overall black species with its long legs and strongly forked tail breeds on islands off Lower California and is unlikely to be confused with the **Ashy Storm-petrel (14)**, a slightly smaller species, sooty black, with edges of upper wing-coverts paler, and under wing-coverts slightly paler. This breeds slightly further north on the Fallaron and Sta Barbara Is. Neither species appears to range far to seaward. **Leach's Storm-petrel (13)** which has an almost universal distribution in all the oceans except the Indian Ocean, breeds on the coasts of western USA, from Lower California northwards to Alaska, and the Aleutian Is ranging far out to sea and so may be observed at intervals at any time along the route, with sooty-black upper parts, greyish-brown upper wing-coverts and sooty-brown underparts. It is distinguished by its white upper tail-coverts with darkish central features, a few whitish feathers on flanks and its forked tail, visible only at close quarters.

Considerably further north, the **Fork-tailed Storm-petrel (14)** which breeds in the Aleutian Is, and on the coasts from southern Alaska, south to Washington, is easily identified by its pearly-grey appearance, palish-white underbody and grey forked tail. It ranges far out to sea but may well be seen closer to the coasts off British Columbia along the route.

ALBATROSSES. At this stage mention must be made of the two North Pacific Albatrosses, the **Black-footed Albatross (6)** which ranges right across the North Pacific from relatively close to the coast, and the **Laysan Albatross (4)**, which also covers the North Pacific; from many observations it appears to join the Black-footed Albatross further to seaward.

The overall sooty-brown plumage of the Black-footed Albatross, with a palish-white area surrounding the base of its bill and extending upwards around its forehead and cheeks behind and below the eyes, its reddish-brown bill, black tail and legs, sometimes showing whitish upper tail-coverts, is easily distinguished. The Laysan Albatross has head, neck, rump and upper tail-coverts white; a dark spot before the eye; back, wings and end of tail dark brown; underparts white, and yellowish-pink bill and legs. Both species are regular ship followers.

MIGRATORY SPECIES. Off the coasts of Washington and British Columbia two contrary currents occur offshore: a cold water current northwards inshore and a slow warm water current south-eastward near the coast of Vancouver Island and along the coast of Southern British Columbia. Here seabirds on migration find an abundance of high surface feed.

Sooty Shearwaters (8) and **Pink-footed Shearwaters (8)** migrate northwards from the south coast of South America crossing the equator from April to June and continue off the west coast of North America and British Columbia where they may be seen in these waters during summer months in considerable flocks. The brownish-black Sooty Shearwater with greyish-brown underparts and pale underwing-coverts differs considerably from the somewhat larger Pink-footed species whose greyish-brown upperparts, white under surface and long massive yellow bill and legs distinguish it.

SKUAS AND PHALAROPES, SABINE'S GULL. Seasonal sightings of the **Arctic Skua (26)**, **Pomarine Skua (26)** and **Long-tailed Skua (26)** also occur close offshore in May and June, and August and September, southward from Alaska, but unlike Phalaropes, which catch the eye in flocks close to the sea, the Skuas tend to fly overhead singly.

Both **Red-necked Phalaropes (25)** and **Grey Phalaropes (25)** are abundant at times along the whole coast of British Columbia during their migration to and from their breeding areas in the high arctic. During the northward migration in May very large flocks, sometimes containing thousands of individuals, may be seen in the environs of Vancouver Island and are abundant along the coast of British Columbia, being seen again during their southward migration from August onwards, from as far north as south of the Alaskan Peninsular.

Pink-footed Shearwater

It is not easy to differentiate between the two species at sea, unless seen at close quarters, owing to their quick movements. In spring plumage the more slender Red-necked Phalarope's slim reddish neck and long slender pointed black bill compares with the reddish underparts, white cheeks and shorter sturdier yellow bill of the grey species.

Mention must be made of the **Sabine's Gull (33, 39)** which breeds in the Arctic regions and migrates southwards in the company of the Phalaropes and may be seen at the same seasons off the western coasts of America, often close offshore. Dark hooded in summer, neck, underparts and forked tail white, it is distinguished by the marked black, grey and white traingles of its upper wing pattern.

A U K S. A number of Auklets, Murrelets, Puffins and the Pigeon Guillemot breed both on the western coasts and on the coasts of Alaska and the Aleutian Is.

Cassin's Auklet (48) breeds along the full length of both coasts from Lower California to the Aleutian Is. It is distinguished by its small size, dusty coloration and conical black bill. **Xantus's Murrelet (48)** and **Craveri's Murrelet (48)** breed on both coasts of Southern California. Both show slate-grey upperparts, Craveri's considerably darker, and white underparts, the latter with dark underwing-coverts.

Further north, **Pigeon Guillemots (46)** nest on small islets from California north to the Aleutian Is and remain close to the coast at sea. They are the Pacific representative of the Black Guillemot but the white area on their flanks is divided by two or three patches of black transverse bars.

The **Marbled Murrelet (48)** is the commonest small auk on the coasts of British Columbia and south-eastern Alaska. It also breeds in Kamchatka, the Kuril Is off eastern Siberia and Vancouver Is. It is distinguished by the white band above the wings, by its sooty-brown upperparts, back and rump barred with buff, underparts blotched white. When swimming it carries its black bill and tail cocked up.

Rhinoceros Auklets (47) breed on many offshore islands from Alaska south to Washington on the American coast, and also on the coast of Kamchatka and the Kuril Is. They are seen commonly off the coasts of British Columbia in summer,

Sabine's Gull

and are distinguished by the blackish horny projection at the base of their rather long orange-yellow bill and white plumes about their heads.

The **Ancient Murrelet (48)** breeds farther north on the Aleutian Is, southern coast of Alaska and Queen Charlotte Is and is seen rarely off the coasts of Vancouver. Its whole head and face are black, a broken white stripe each side of crown. The upperparts are slaty-blue, and the sides of the neck and the underparts white.

Tufted Puffins (47) breed from eastern Siberia through the Aleutian Is to Alaska and down the American coast to Sta Barbara, California and are frequently seen off the coasts. They are very distinctive birds, with their sooty-black to sooty-brown overall plumage offset by elongated yellow tufts on the sides of the head, a very large bill, red at tip, olive-green at base, and bright red legs.

The **Horned Puffin (47)** ranges more northerly than other species mentioned, and breeds on the arctic coast of eastern Siberia to Cape Lisburne, Alaska, southwards to Aleutian Is. Distinguished by its black upperparts, white cheeks which are white in summer, and grey in winter, white underparts, lack of plumes on head, and, particularly, by its very large reddish triangular bill, light yellow at base. Unlikely to be seen close to the coast.

Should the ship be visiting the harbours of San Francisco and Vancouver during its passage a number of species are likely to be seen.

San Francisco harbour

CORMORANTS, GULLS, AUKS. Within the harbour **Brandt's Cormorant (21)**, the commonest cormorant on the Pacific West Coast of America, is sure to be seen. A large cormorant with its glossy greenish-black plumage, it is distinguished by the fawn-coloured throat; naked skin of face and throat blue; the throat feathers extend forward to a point.

The **Double-crested Cormorant (21)** also occurs and is distinguished by tufts of black and white curly feathers on each side of head in summer plumage; and orange-yellow area on face.

Not all seabirds will be seen at all seasons, for some are on passage or wintering from more distant breeding areas. Close inshore the gulls will attract attention first.

A number of **Western Gulls (27, 34)** breed locally and will be seen in the inner reaches of the harbour. They can be distinguished from the very similar Herring Gull by the darked, leaden-grey mantle, and from the **Californian Gull (28, 35)** by their flesh-coloured legs. This latter gull has a medium-grey mantle, like the Herring Gull, and greenish-yellow legs. It breeds on inland lakes in western North America and occurs on the coast and in harbours more often in autumn and winter.

The **Common** or **Short-billed Gull** and the **Ring-billed Gull (28, 35, 40)** both breed inland on lakes in Canada and the northern United States but may occur as winter migrants occasionally. The same may be said of **Bonaparte's Gull (31, 36)**, which also breeds in the interior of Alaska and western Canada, but might be seen on migration southwards to winter on the coasts of Mexico and Gulf of Panama. Yet another, **Heerman's Gull (30, 38)** which breeds on the coasts of Mexico migrates north in winter as far as Vancouver. Head and upper neck white in summer, brownish in winter, mantle slate-coloured, underparts and tail-coverts grey and tail dull black. Bill red, legs black.

Vancouver Island and roadsteads

Several of the species already quoted earlier or under San Francisco also occur at Vancouver Island and environs.

Northern Fulmar (11).

Pelagic Cormorant (21). The smallest cormorant in the North Pacific and commonest on coast of British Columbia; overall greenish-black with large white patch on each flank. Throat and pouch coral red, tufts of bronze feathers on crown and nape when breeding.

Glaucous-winged Gull (29, 35). Breeds locally and also seen frequently offshore.

Western Gull (27, 34), a regular winter visitor.

California Gull (28, 35), occurs periodically.

Common or **Short-billed Gull (28, 35, 40)**, confined to beaches and inlets.

Bonaparte's Gull (31, 36), migrates up west coast from early May to mid June. Seen most frequently along the east coast of Vancouver Island and throughout length of Johnstone Strait in August.

Pigeon Guillemot (46), almost entirely resident, nesting on small islets.

Marbled Murrelet (48), occurs regularly on all inshore waters, and restricted to inlets.

Ancient Murrelet (48). Restricted to inshore waters and seen frequently during summer months.

Rhinoceros Auklet (47) breeds on many offshore islets, commonly seen all summer.

Tufted Puffin (47) breeds on several islands, particularly Solander Island.

Onwards to the Bering Sea

Off the coast of Vancouver a cold inshore north-westerly current flows. Sometimes the tail end of the warmer West Wind Drift, which normally flows south-easterly at a considerable distance to seaward, creates a convergence and turbulence closer inshore, providing an area of rich plankton feed where oceanic seabirds gather. For this reason, many of the seabirds either on migration or dispersing southwards in winter from higher latitudes occur at no great distance from the coast. An interesting aspect is the diversity of species to be seen at different seasons, and not all species will be seen during a single voyage.

MIGRATING GULLS. **Sabine's Gull (33, 39)**. This strikingly patterned gull breeds in high arctic latitudes but travels up and down the coast during its long seasonal migrations, wintering along the west coast of S. America. It may be seen frequently both inshore and well offshore in May and June, and later on southward migration from August onwards.

Bonaparte's Gull (31, 36). These gulls appear to migrate northwards along the coast from early May to mid-June and later in August to and from inland breeding grounds.

Heermann's Gull (30, 38). Heermann's Gull breeds southwards from the Gulf of California, but some disperse northwards after breeding and may be seen along the coast from late July onwards. In summer the distinctive white heads and upper-necks in adults against the otherwise overall grey plumage helps identification.

Common Kittiwake (33, 39). The Common Kittiwake occurs off the coast principally on passage to northerly breeding areas between March and May, after which immature non-breeding birds are still likely to be seen.

CORMORANTS. The **Pelagic Cormorant (21)**. This small dark glossy-green cormorant is a very common sight close inshore at all seasons. **Brandt's Cormorant (21)**, frequently seen offshore, is larger than the Pelagic Cormorant showing a fawn patch on the throat.

AUKS. Outside the breeding season, these species remain at sea, and of the seven species which occur off the coast, perhaps the **Pigeon Guillemot (46)** and the **Marbled Murrelet (48)** are those most likely to be seen close inshore. The **Common Guillemot (46)**, **Rhinoceros Auklet (47)**, **Tufted Puffin (47)**, **Cassin's Auklet (48)**, **Ancient Murrelet (48)**, **Horned Puffin (47)** and **Parakeet Auklet (48)** have all been recorded.

The start of the voyage

Before land and islands disappear from sight a number of oceanic species including migratory species to be described later are likely to be observed. **Northern Fulmars (11)** may be seen in small numbers at all seasons but increase in winter months. Both fulmars and **Fork-tailed Storm-petrels (14)** follow fishing vessels, favouring the cold water off the coast. Both are likely to be seen however throughout the voyage. The Fork-tailed Storm-petrel with its pearly-grey upperparts, pale grey underparts and grey forked tail is easily distinguishable from the **Leach's Storm-petrel (13)** which has a generally sooty-brown plumage and, in the northern races, an oval white rump patch divided by a few dark feathers. Leach's Storm-petrel is less commonly seen, and ranges throughout the ocean usually further to seaward.

Soon the first **Black-footed Albatross (6)** will pick up the ship. They are always more numerous than the **Laysan Albatross (4)** and more bold in approaching close astern of ships. Both species breed in the Hawaiian Is. from October to July, dispersing northwards outside the breeding season. Laysan Albatrosses do not appear to extend their range so close to the N. American coast and are likely to be seen somewhat later in the voyage.

At sea towards the Aleutian Islands

GLOBE-SPANNING MIGRANTS, SEASONAL SIGHTINGS. **Sooty** and **Pink-footed Shearwaters (8)**. In the eastern Pacific both species migrate northwards up the west coast of S. America on completion of their breeding seasons, Sooty Shearwaters in considerably larger numbers. Sooty Shearwaters appear to commence migration somewhat earlier but both species are crossing the Equator from April to June. The movement continues close off the west coast of N. America, and flocks of Sooty Shearwaters should be looked for at the start of the voyage off the coast from April, lesser numbers of Pink-footed Shearwaters from June onwards. Sooty Shearwaters appear to swing westwards between 45° and 55°N. until August. Flocks of 200 or more have been observed at 50°N., 145°W. and again at 45°N. between 170° and 175°W. in September when commencing their return journey. These shearwaters doubtless converge in mid-ocean with similar western Pacific species which have migrated from breeding quarters in New Zealand. **Short-tailed Shearwaters (8)** from the Bass Strait reach the Bering Sea spreading east to overlap with Sooty Shearwaters in the south of the Aleutian Is.

Pink-footed Shearwaters do not appear to spread so far west but have been observed between 50° and 55°N. south-east of the Aleutian Is. in August, starting to return in September when they may be seen again close offshore in Vancouver waters. The larger heavily built Pink-footed Shearwater shows brownish-grey upperparts, white underbody and a long massive yellow bill. It should not be difficult to distinguish from the smaller blackish-brown Sooty Shearwater which shows a greyish-brown underbody, silvery central linings to its dark underwings and a slender black bill. The slower deliberate flight of the Pink-footed species contrasts with the swifter banking, arcing and gliding flight of the Sooty.

PHALAROPES. Two species of these tiny delicate waders which breed in the high arctic migrate outside the breeding season to winter off the west coast of S. America in the Humboldt Current. Observed at sea, often resting in small flocks on the surface, it is rarely possible to differentiate between the species. **Red-necked Phalaropes (25)** migrate along the west coast of N. America and flocks are likely to be seen off the coast of British Columbia on northward migration in May and again on southward migration from mid-July onwards. **Grey Phalaropes (25)** follow a similar pattern but appear to be less plentiful along the coast. They have been observed at sea covering a broad front between 30°N. and 40°N. and between 150° and 170°W. both in spring and autumn.

SKUAS. **Great, Arctic, Pomarine** and **Long-tailed Skuas (26)**. Although the three smaller species, also commonly known as jaegers, cross the route during their trans-equatorial migrations, the opportunity for sightings is usually infrequent. Unlike shearwaters or phalaropes which tend to catch the eye low over the sea, skuas usually pass overhead singly. Pomarine and Long-tailed Skuas are more likely to be seen off the coast of British Columbia between May/June and August/September, but they have been observed occasionally far out at sea as far as the Aleutian Is. on migration. Great Skuas have been recorded by observers in the Canadian Ocean Weather Ship at Station Papa, 50°N., 145°W. during summer months.

Seabirds naturally collect around stationary Weather Ships on the lookout for pickings cast overboard. A recent summary of observations made from such a ship at Station Papa may serve as a guide to species liable to be seen during the mid-ocean passage towards the Aleutian Is. A ship on passage will not expect to see the numbers quoted at any one time.

During the summer months at this station from May to September, Black-footed Albatrosses were present in groups of sometimes up to 70 birds. Laysan Albatrosses occurred only singly or in pairs. Northern Fulmars were constantly in evidence in groups of up to 20, almost all in the dark phase. Fork-tailed Storm-petrels were always present in small numbers, equally active by day and night, frequently landing on board at night. In June a few dark shearwaters were seen, later in August to be confirmed as Sooty Shearwaters, when flocks numbered over 200 at one time. In June and again in August and September an occasional Great Skua, Pomarine and Long-tailed Skuas were seen, and more frequently **Arctic Terns (41, 42)**. During these months **Glaucous Gulls (29, 35, 40)** and Glaucous-winged Gulls were absent from the ocean, and apart from a few Tufted Puffins, of which large flocks may be seen close off the Aleutian Is. at this season, there was an absence of other members of the Alcidae family.

Later in November and December, while Black-footed Albatrosses had almost disappeared, Laysan Albatrosses were more common. Northern Fulmars remained in evidence, and Glaucous-winged Gulls in groups of 20 or more. Occasionally **Common Kittiwakes (33, 39)** and Glaucous Gulls put in an appearance.

The Aleutian Islands and Bering Sea

Enclosed by the bleak rocky coasts of the long curving chain of the Aleutian Is. to the south, the coast of western Alaska to the east, north-eastern Siberia and Kamchatka to the west, the Bering Sea and its islands provide the breeding and feeding area for an abundance of species. The Bering Sea is comparable both in climate and oceanic food with the conditions prevailing in the sub-antarctic islands. On these fog-bound islands and coasts breeding colonies of Northern Fulmars, Fork-tailed Storm-petrels, Leach's Storm-petrels, **Pelagic** and **Red-faced Cormorants (21)**, Glaucous-winged Gulls, **Herring Gulls (28, 35, 40)**, Slaty-backed Gulls (27, 34), Common Kittiwakes and **Red-legged Kittiwakes (33, 39)** abound.

The Alcidae are particularly well represented: **Brunnich's Guillemot (46)**, **Horned Puffin (47)**, **Crested** and **Whiskered Auklets (47)**, **Parakeet Auklet (48)**, **Least Auklet (47, 48)**, **Kittlitz's Murrelet (48)** and the Ancient Murrelet all breed within the area. Others such as the Marbled Murrelet, Rhinoceros Auklet, Pigeon Guillemot, Common Guillemot, Tufted Puffin and Cassin's Auklet extend their breeding range further south. The **Spectacled Guillemot (46)** is more restricted to the Asiatic coast.

Unfortunately, the frequently foul weather conditions make observation of these small alcids difficult; fleeting glimpses cause uncertain identifications.

Still further north in arctic regions the **Ivory Gull (33, 39)** and Glaucous Gull, the Arctic Tern, Pomarine and Long-tailed Skuas, and the Red-necked and Grey Phalaropes breed. The **Common Tern (41, 43)**, **Aleutian Tern (44)** and Arctic Skua breed as far south as the Aleutians.

In addition to these breeding residents and passage migrants, the Laysan Albatross has been observed within the Bering Sea, and in the late summer months flocks of Sooty Shearwaters penetrate the Bering Sea at the termination of their vast trans-equatorial migration from their breeding quarters in New Zealand.

Observers known to the author in ships which have passed through the Bering Sea have been few and far between but from a study of their reports it appears that Northern Fulmars, Brunnich's Guillemots, Tufted Puffins, Horned Puffins, Crested Auklets, Common Kittiwakes and Red-legged Kittiwakes have been seen

Crested Auklet

most frequently; phalaropes and Pomarine Skuas in August, and in addition in January Glaucous and Glaucous-winged Gulls and on one occasion an Ivory Gull.

Members of the Alcidae family, with their habit of diving immediately on being disturbed, are notably difficult to identify under the conditions of weather and visibility which obtain so often in the Bering Sea. One can but suggest to an observer approaching the Bering Sea that previous study of the salient points of difference (shown in the plates of the Field Guide) of the great variety of this family would increase "just that chance" of identifying an otherwise doubtful species.

Route to Arctic waters

Ships and deep water fishing vessels cross the Arctic Circle from the open waters of the N. Atlantic Ocean whether it be to Iceland, Spitsbergen, or round the North Cape towards Murmansk or Archangel. There is less cause for them to do so from the N. Pacific Ocean through the narrow waters of the Bering Strait.

Although the author has received records of observations of seabirds from ships on passage to and from Murmansk, the direct route to the arctic now described is largely built up at the outset from the day to day reporting of British Ocean Weather Ships over a period of several years. From an analysis of these reports, covering every month in the years, a pattern of the oceanic distribution of the seabirds in the N. Atlantic between latitudes 55°N. and 65°N. and 15°W. to 30°W. has become evident. The probability of observing seabirds on the route selected must be related to some extent to these findings together with records from ships which have penetrated north of 70°N., and are therefore summarised briefly by species as the route is covered.

The route presupposes a ship outward bound from a northern port in the west of the British Isles, steering to pass east of Iceland, thence onwards past Jan Mayen to the southern limit of the polar ice.

Ocean weather ship stations referred to

Station Alpha, 62°N., 33°W., some 300 miles west by south of Iceland. Station India, 59°N., 19°W., some 250 miles south of Iceland. Station Juliet, 52°N., 25°W., some 350 miles west by south of Ireland.

Outward Bound to the North

Many seabirds breed on islands off the west coast of Scotland and on the Hebrides, and if the ship is passing close to the islands during the breeding season, any of the species listed below may be seen. **Northern Fulmars (11)**, **Manx Shearwaters (9)**, **British** and **Leach's Storm-petrels (13)**, **Northern Gannets (18)**, **Great** and **Arctic Skuas (26)**, **Common Cormorants (20, 23)**, **Shags (21)**, **Great Black-backed** and **Lesser Black-backed Gulls (27, 34, 40)**, **Herring** and **Common Gulls (28, 35, 40)**, **Northern Black-headed Gulls (28, 31, 32, 37, 40)**, **Common Kittiwakes (33, 39)**, **Common** and **Arctic Terns (41, 42, 43)**, and the three species of auks, **Common Guillemots (46)**, **Razorbills (46)** and **Atlantic Puffins (47)**. The **Black Guillemot (46)** clings close to the coastline and is unlikely to be seen.

Once in the open ocean many species will be left behind and the opportunities of sighting certain species varies with the seasons of the year. It is noticeable however that between the British Isles and Iceland seabirds tend to follow ships; even the most inshore gulls, Great Black-backed, Lesser Black-backed and Herring Gulls, have been reported by ships throughout the passage. They have become accustomed to following and collecting around fishing vessels where offal is always present when nets are hauled, and it is around these ships and Ocean Weather Ships

Fulmar and Northern Gannet

that the sight of gulls amongst the large flocks of fulmars, petrels and kittiwakes occurs chiefly.

In the open ocean fulmars and kittiwakes may be seen regularly over the whole route to Iceland, the fulmars almost entirely pale phase birds. Both fulmars and kittiwakes are at peak numbers between November and May, fulmars usually outnumbering kittiwakes slightly. While there is a slight withdrawal of fulmars from May to September, considerable numbers are always to be seen in the open ocean. On the other hand an almost complete withdrawal of kittiwakes occurs between the end of May and the end of July, breeding birds foraging for food closer to their breeding cliffs.

Northern Gannets may be seen at intervals, usually singly, over this part of the route at all seasons. Lesser Black-backed Gulls and occasionally Herring Gulls will follow ships although these gulls are frequently absent from June to August from available records. Guillemots, Razorbills and puffins have been observed by ships well out at sea. The **Little Auk (46)**, which breeds in millions in the high arctic, is more oceanic, dispersing southwards during autumn and winter months, and a lookout should be kept for this very small stubby black and white auk.

Seasonal migrations

To a traveller on this route to arctic waters the pattern of seasonal migrations of certain migrants as observed from the ocean weather stations may provide the best guide. Reports from these ships disclose a generally consistent pattern.

Great Shearwaters (9). A clockwise movement begins with a very few birds appearing at Alpha in July, so small that it seems probable that this is the extreme northerly limit of this species. Further to the east and south at India somewhat larger numbers begin to appear in August, and further south still at Juliet large concentrations have occurred in September and October, none being recorded after October.

Sooty Shearwaters (8). Only isolated birds have reached Alpha by late June, a few at India in late July and August, and similarly relatively small numbers at Juliet in September and October. None after October.

Manx Shearwaters (9). None have ever been reported as far north and west as Alpha, and they have only been recorded in small numbers, less than ten in a month (March), at India. They have been known to appear at Juliet in March and April, perhaps following an easterly course towards their breeding islands in the British Isles.

STORM-PETRELS. Storm-petrels are frequently difficult to identify during the high winds and seas so prevalent at the weather stations. **British Storm-petrels (13)** have been reported rarely with certainty; **Leach's Storm-petrels (13)** only once at Alpha in June, and once or twice at India in September, Probably their most northerly limit. **Wilson's Storm-petrels (13)** have however reached the furthest south station Juliet from August to October, on one occasion in considerable numbers.

A ship on the route is therefore likely to be too far to the east and north to sight shearwaters and petrels with the possible exception of Leach's Storm-petrel.

SKUAS. The northward and southward migration of all four skuas has been observed with great regularity at all three weather stations. In the western quarter at Alpha the northward passage occurs between mid-May and early June. **Pomarine Skuas (26)** predominate with lesser numbers of **Long-tailed Skuas (26)**, Great Skuas and Arctic Skuas. In the eastern quarter at Juliet and India the passage occurs somewhat earlier in late April and May. Great Skuas predominate with Pomarine Skuas and Long-tailed Skuas in lesser numbers. In all cases Arctic Skuas appear in numbers. The southward passage occurs between mid-August and early October.

It is clear however from ship records that the skuas also migrate further to the east, and a ship on the route may well expect to observe skuas at the appropriate seasons.

Iceland and Jan Mayen

Very large colonies of fulmars, gannets, **Brunnich's Guillemots (46)**, Common Guillemots, Razorbills, puffins, Little Auks, and smaller numbers of Black Guillemots, Great Black-backed Gulls, Herring Gulls and **Glaucous Gulls (29, 35, 40)** breed in Iceland. Here also the Great Skua, Arctic Skua, **Red-necked** and **Grey Phalaropes (25)** and Arctic Tern will be found breeding. The skuas, phalaropes and Arctic Terns occur only as early summer breeding migrants and by August will be starting their long southerly migrations.

Between the latitudes of Iceland and Jan Mayen, several species have been observed far out at sea midway between the land and the Norwegian coast. Fulmars and kittiwakes are seen regularly. Great Black-backed Gulls and Herring Gulls frequently, and Glaucous Gulls and puffins are not uncommon. The Little Auk sometimes occurs in flocks. More surprising have been confirmed sightings of Common Gulls and a Northern Gannet north of 70°N. The **Iceland Gull (33, 40)** which breeds in Greenland is less likely to be seen.

Great Skua and Storm-petrel

Northwards to the ice edge

Northwards in the Greenland Sea the number of seabirds decreases until west of Spitsbergen where such arctic breeding species as the Northern Fulmar, Arctic Skua, Glaucous Gull, Common Kittiwake, **Ivory** and **Sabine's Gulls (33, 39)**, Arctic Tern, Little Auk, Brunnich's Guillemot, Black Guillemot and puffin breed. An indication of the seabirds observed by members of the Royal Naval Birdwatching Society in ships carrying out cold weather trials between April and June up to 80°N. concludes this passage. Fulmars and kittiwakes occurred in the open sea and over leads in the pack ice. Glaucous Gulls were common over open water up to 78°N., and on one occasion a Great Black-backed Gull was seen on the pack ice at 79.5°N. Ivory Gulls have been seen occasionally, singly or in groups of two or three, flying over the pack ice. Arctic Skuas, on one occasion a Pomarine Skua, and a Great Skua have also been observed near the pack edge. Brunnich's Guillemots and Black Guillemots were common over open pools, and a puffin occurred north of 79.5°N.

Amongst observations of Little Auks, of which small flocks were observed over the pack ice, two unusual incidents are worthy of note. On one occasion in calm weather, a glassy sea surrounding the ship, a Little Auk could be seen swimming under water at a depth of some ten metres. On a different occasion the following unique observation was recorded by a different class of ship.

"On 4th March when we were submerged 150 ft (46 metres), below 10 ft (3 metres) of ice, a bird was seen swimming under water amongst a few fish and jellyfish in a considerable concentration of plankton. Viewed through the high-powered periscope its colours were hard to assess, but the bird had every appearance of a Little Auk and could hardly have been of any other species. Two days later we surfaced within an ice lead and identified an Ivory Gull. Later, while observing two Bearded Seals, a Snow Bunting alighted on the fore-casing, eventually to fly off towards Greenland. Ahead stretched ice as far as the eye could see."

Route to Antarctica

Port Stanley in the Falkland Is. has frequently been the departure point for ships carrying supplies to antarctic bases during the southern summer months. The route described envisages a passage in January from the Falkland Is. to S. Georgia, and onwards through the Weddell Sea to a landfall at the ice shelf of the antarctic continent, a route which varies according to the vicissitudes of the pack ice.

A great wealth and variety of oceanic seabirds breed in the sub-antarctic islands surrounding the approaches to the Weddell Sea, and a narrative can but give a pattern of the different species which may be seen almost daily. A day to day record would tend to become monotonous.

References to the illustrations of species quoted are listed at the close of the Route.

The Falkland Islands

A great many seabirds breed on the islands, amongst them; Gentoo, Macaroni, Rock-hopper and Magellan Penguins, which may be seen on the shore line and beaches; Black-browed and Grey-headed Albatrosses; Giant, White-chinned and Blue Petrels; Thick-billed Prions; Great and Sooty Shearwaters; Wilson's and Grey-backed Storm-petrels; Common Diving-petrels; Magellan and King Cormorants; Southern Black-backed and Magellan Gulls; Patagonian Black-headed Gulls and South American Terns.

The Falkland Islands to South Georgia

King Cormorants and Southern Black-backed Gulls may accompany the ship until two or three miles offshore; later Wandering and Black-browed Albatrosses, Giant Petrels and Pintado Petrels are likely to pick up the ship and be in close attendance. Others may appear, taking less notice of the ship, Grey-headed Albatrosses, Sooty Shearwaters and a passing Southern Fulmar. During the passage additional species must be looked for, White-chinned Petrels and Wilson's Storm-petrels following astern, a Southern Great Skua, Blue Petrels and prions often in considerable flocks. Viewed thus as they bank and zigzag low over the sea exposing their blue-grey blacks at one moment and white underparts an instant later it is no easy matter to differentiate between them. Both the Blue Petrels and prions show dark inverted W bands across the upperwing-coverts, but the Blue Petrels have square entirely white tails, while the prions show a black band at the outer end of their wedge-shaped tails. Infrequently Black-bellied Storm-petrels may be seen following astern with their noticeable hopping and fluttering flight.

As S. Georgia is approached more seabirds will appear. The island is spectacular, its snow-covered mountains leading down to lower slopes where great colonies of albatrosses nest; the Light-mantled Sooty Albatross prefers to nest on ledges on the cliffs, where also in holes, crannies and burrows the petrels, storm-petrels and prions breed.

White-chinned Petrel

The harbour at Cumberland Bay may often be teeming with a motley collection of oceanic birds; the incessant chattering of Pintado Petrels, squabbling Giant Petrels, albatrosses joining the fray, moaning and braying over gash thrown overboard, and little Wilson's Storm-petrels dancing with long legs dangling. Along the shore line Chin-strap Penguins, Blue-eyed Cormorants, and Southern Black-backed Gulls occupy the rocks. The Blue-eyed Cormorants have a curious affinity for ships, frequently flying towards them and indeed sometimes deliberately landing on board. The curious Yellow-billed Sheathbill also breeds on S. Georgia and has been known to land on ships too, but is certainly an unlikely arrival.

Southwards from South Georgia

At the outset there will be little change from species already seen. Perhaps a few King Penguins may be seen 'porpoising' at sea; Georgian Diving-petrels, Blue Petrels, prions and always the Wandering, Black-browed and now Light-mantled Sooty Albatrosses, White-chinned and Pintado Petrels. Passing between the S. Orkney and S. Sandwich Is. changes are likely. Already the ship will have passed belts of brash and growlers scattered over the sea, and the first white Snow Petrels may be seen. They breed on S. Georgia and abundantly on the S. Orkney and S. Sandwich Is. and on the antarctic continent.

Later, as the ship steams south, albatrosses and Giant Petrels will begin to disappear; prions and Wilson's Storm-petrel, and occasional Southern Fulmar, Kerguelen Petrel and southern Great Skua may still be seen. Groups of Adelie Penguins, which breed on the S. Orkney and S. Sandwich Is. and on the antarctic continent itself, are seen frequently far out at sea on the pack ice. It is no uncommon sight to see the great Emperor Penguins also, standing head and shoulders above the little Adelies. In the background, flat topped icebergs, which have broken from the continental ice cliffs, will be drifting slowly northwards and here and there Weddell and Crabeater seals may be seen basking on the ice.

Antarctic Petrel

Before the ship crosses the Antarctic Circle (66.5°S.) the albatrosses will have gone and new birds will appear. Snow Petrels, already seen, are likely to increase in numbers and Antarctic Petrels will appear, clearly identified by the white patches on their brown upperwings, the brown tips of their white tails and their white underparts. As the ship sights the long line of the high coastal ice cliffs Antarctic Terns may be seen. Flocks of all three species are quite a common sight, but less likely the paler McCormick's Skua, the most southerly race of all the skua family.

Along the shore line beyond the ice cliffs stretches the shelf ice, alongside which supply ships may secure. Here inquisitive Adelie Penguins sometimes provide a small reception committee, and during the winter darkness the Emperor Penguins incubate their single eggs. The ship will have reached 75°36′S., some 900 miles from the South Pole. At midnight in January the sun will still ride well above the horizon.

SPECIES QUOTED. **King, Emperor, Gentoo, Adelie, Chin-strap** and **Magellan Penguins (1), Rock-hopper** and **Macaroni Penguins (2), Wandering Albatross (3), Black-browed** and **Grey-headed Albatrosses (5), Light-mantled Sooty Albatross (6), Giant Petrel (6, 7), Pintado Petrel (11), Southern Fulmar (11), Blue, Snow, Kerguelen** and **Antarctic Petrels (11), prions** sp. **(11), White-chinned Petrel (7), Sooty Shearwater (8), Wilson's (13), Grey-backed (14)** and **Black-bellied Storm-petrels (13), Georgian Diving-petrel (14), Magellan** and **Blue-eyed Cormorants (22), King Cormorant (p. 78), Yellow-billed Sheathbill (25),** southern **Great** and **McCormick's Skua (26), Magellan Gull (30, 38), Southern Black-backed Gull (27, 34, 40), Patagonian Black-headed Gull (31, 36), Antarctic Tern (42)** and **South American Tern (42).**

The Seabirds of Antarctica

The antarctic continent

With the exception of the northern "bill" of the antarctic peninsula, almost the entire coastline of the antarctic continent lies within 20° of the latitude of the South Pole. For four months of the year from the middle of April until the middle of August the sun never rises above the horizon, and save for the light shed by the moon the continent is virtually clothed in darkness. Through the month of May for example an average temperature of 65° of frost has been recorded in places, with individual temperatures as low as 90° of frost, accompanied by winds and snow blizzards of great intensity. The seaward walls of the great ice cliffs, some 200 ft in height, cling to the coastline, and the fast ice stretches outwards as far as the eye can see. At this season only the **Emperor Penguin (1)** broods its eggs, and such seabirds as may appear later are absent.

The main antarctic continent is covered perpetually in snow, but in the summer months from October to March along certain warmer coastlines pleasantly calm sunny weather often prevails, and here a scale-like lichen may be found growing on the rocks. In such localities, by October when the fast ice breaks from the shore, plankton multiplies immensely under the summer sun and krill abounds. Beyond the pack ice the sea is rich in fish and krill, and oceanic seabirds move in.

Not all venture as far as the pack ice, but recent surveys have thrown new light upon the southerly limits in which certain species may be seen – and some have come to breed on the continent.

Seabirds breeding on the antarctic mainland

PENGUINS. Emperor Penguins breed in colonies, usually on the ice shelf, in many localities around the mainland, and do not disperse beyond the pack ice outside their breeding season. Their egg demands such a prolonged incubation period that adults come to shore in March or April to breed during winter darkness, the males incubating the eggs while the females remain at sea until the chicks are hatching. The chicks hatch in July when the females relieve the males which leave for the sea. By November or December the young are usually ready to take to the sea. In the case of the **Adelie Penguins (1)** the incubation period is only half that of the Emperor Penguins, and it is not until October that they may be seen swimming to the coast to leap onto the ice and march towards their breeding colonies. The birds usually leave the coast again in April to spend the non-breeding season amongst the pack ice.

PETRELS. **Antarctic** and **Snow Petrels (11)** breed regularly on the continent, favouring ice free cliffs frequently some distance inland. The **Giant Petrel (6, 7)**, the **Southern Fulmar (11)** and **Pintado Petrel (11)** are known to breed in Adelie Land, and probably in other localities in the Australian Antarctic Territory, favouring rock ledges on headlands or islands, or even the gravelly shore line in these warmer zones. Except for the Giant Petrel, the four smaller petrels arrive during the second half of October, adults and young leaving at the end of April or May.

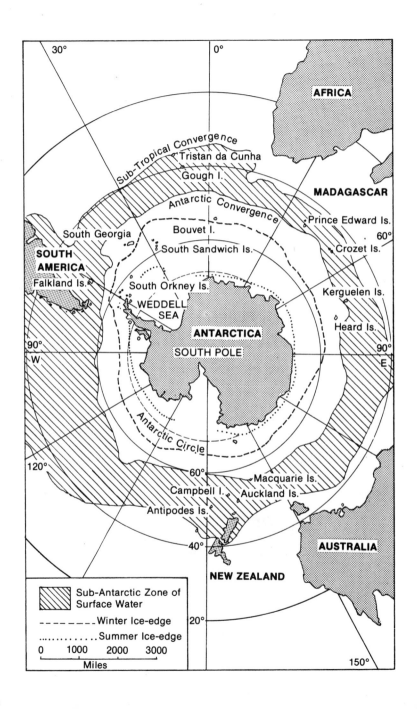

30°

0°

AFRICA

Sub-Tropical Convergence

Tristan da Cunha

Gough I.

MADAGASCAR

Antarctic Convergence

Prince Edward Is.

South Georgia

Bouvet I.

60°

SOUTH AMERICA

South Sandwich Is.

Crozet Is.

Falkland Is.

South Orkney Is.

Kerguelen Is.

WEDDELL SEA

Heard Is.

90° W

ANTARCTICA

SOUTH POLE

90° E

Antarctic Circle

120°

60°

Macquarie Is.

Campbell I.

Auckland Is.

Antipodes Is.

40°

AUSTRALIA

NEW ZEALAND

20°

	Sub-Antarctic Zone of Surface Water
- - - - -	Winter Ice-edge
....	Summer Ice-edge

0   1000   2000   3000

Miles

150°

STORM-PETRELS. **Wilson's Storm-petrel (13)** is the only species to breed on the continent. It has been recorded reaching Wilkes Land in November, and favours crevices under rocks in which to nest.

SKUAS. **McCormick's Skua (26)** is the sole member of the skua family to breed on the continent, arriving in October, adults and young leaving again at the beginning of April. McCormick's Skua, together with the Giant Petrel, prey on young of other breeding species and scavenge for all manner of offal.

The antarctic peninsula

Both the Emperor and Adelie Penguins breed in colonies on the peninsula in smaller numbers, the Adelie extending its range to large colonies on the S. Orkney and S. Sandwich Is. Other species also breed on the peninsula and its islands, and, if we include Elephant I., we find the **Gentoo** and **Chin-strap Penguins (1)**, the **Macaroni Penguin (2)**, the **Snow Petrel**, Wilson's Storm-petrel, **Black-bellied Storm-petrel (13)**, the Giant Petrel, Pintado Petrel, **Dove Prion (11)**, **Blue-eyed Cormorant (22)**, **Yellow-billed Sheathbill (25)**, **Southern Black-backed Gull (27, 34, 40)** and the **Antarctic Tern (41)**.

The seas around Antarctica

The Antarctic Convergence extends around the antarctic continent from 30°W. eastwards through Kerguelen Is. at 50°S., thence towards Macquarie I. at about 55°S., thereafter following westwards at about 60°S. to the tip of the antarctic peninsula, finally regaining 50°S. again.

The seabirds described are not necessarily confined within the Antarctic Convergence; they include those which have been observed to penetrate between approximately 60°S. and the limit of the seaward edge of the pack ice.

The edge of the pack ice varies in its latitude between the antarctic winter and summer months, and moves unpredictably with wind and weather. Records from

Emperor Penguin

British antarctic supply ships entering the Weddell Sea area between December and February have shown the seaward edge of the pack ice being met on average between 60°S. and 64°S., but there are occasions when wide areas of open water may approach much closer to land during the antarctic summer.

Apart from those species which breed on the continent, and later take to sea, other seabirds, whose oceanic range may also extend far north of the Antarctic Convergence, do not penetrate the pack ice. They may however exploit open leads within the pack.

No definite boundaries confine the movements of these seabirds, but from observations obtained thus far a general pattern emerges.

Seabirds which range outwards from the antarctic continent and rarely exceed the seaward limits of the pack ice

Emperor Penguin, Adelie Penguin. The Adelie Penguin also breeds in great numbers on the S. Orkney, S. Shetland and S. Sandwich Is., and birds from these islands may be seen between the islands and the pack. Snow Petrel, infrequently seen more than 30 miles to seaward on the ice edge. Antarctic Tern, usually met with within 15 miles of the pack ice.

Seabirds which may range within 50 miles of the outer ice edge

Antarctic Petrel, Southern Fulmar, Pintado Petrel, Giant Petrel, **Kerguelen Petrel (11)**, Wilson's Storm-petrel, McCormick's Skua, southern Great Skua.

Seabirds which range southwards and occasionally reach the pack ice

Wandering Albatross (3), Light-mantled Sooty Albatross (6), White-headed and **Blue Petrels (11), White-chinned Petrel (7), Peale's Petrel** (possibly) **(12)**, those Snow Petrels which breed on the S. Orkney and S. Sandwich Is., Dove Prion and Arctic Tern.

Seabirds observed to penetrate to or slightly south of 60°S.

Black-browed Albatross, Grey-headed Albatross.

The sea surface waters surrounding the outer edge of the pack ice in southern summer months contain a quantity of planktonic organisms and fish, providing an ideal feeding area for southern oceanic seabirds. It may be expected that as more ships penetrate the seas around Antarctica and observations of seabirds continue, the summary above will be added to.

● indicates breeding is confirmed
– indicates that a species may breed but this is not confirmed

Seabirds breeding on principal islands in central Pacific Ocean, **north of the Equator**. *Note*: other non-breeding species not quoted but may be seen in the vicinity.

	Hawaiian Is	Line Is	Wake Is	Marshall Is	Gilbert Is & Ocean Is	Caroline Is	Mariana Is	Bonin Volcano Is	Torishima I
Black-footed Albatross	●	–	–	–	–	–	–	–	
Laysan Albatross	●	–	–	–	–	–	–	–	
Hawaiian Petrel	●	–	–	–	–	–	–	–	
Bonin Petrel	●	–	–	–	–	–	–	●	
Bulwer's Petrel	●	–	–	–	–	–	–	●	
Wedge-tailed Shearwater	●	●	–	●	–	●	●	●	
Christmas Shearwater	●	●	–	–	–	–	–	–	
Newell's Shearwater	●	–	–	–	–	–	–	–	
Tristram's Storm-petrel	●	–	–	–	–	–	–	●	
Madeiran Storm-petrel	●	–	–	–	–	–	–	–	
Red-tailed Tropic-bird	●	●	●	●	–	–	●	●	
White-tailed Tropic-bird	●	●	●	●	●	●	●	–	
Blue-faced Booby	●	●	–	●	–	–	●	–	
Brown Booby	●	●	●	●	●	●	●	●	
Red-footed Booby	●	●	●	●	●	●	●	–	
Great Frigate-bird	●	●	●	●	–	●	–	–	
Sooty Tern	●	●	●	●	●	●	●	●	
Spectacled Tern	●	●	●	●	●	–	–	–	
Blue-grey Noddy	●	●	–	●	–	–	–	–	
Brown Noddy	●	●	●	●	●	●	●	●	
White-capped Noddy	●	●	–	●	●	●	●	●	
White Tern	●	●	–	●	●	–	●	●	
Audubon's Shearwater	–	●	–	–	–	●	●	●	
Phoenix Petrel	–	●	–	–	–	–	–	–	
White-throated Storm-petrel	–	●	–	–	–	–	–	–	
Lesser Frigate-bird	–	●	–	–	–	–	–	–	
Crested Tern	–	●	–	●	●	●	–	●	
Black-naped Tern	–		–	●	●	●	–	–	
Matsudaira's Storm-petrel	–	–	–	–	–	–	–	●	
Short-tailed or Stellar's Albatross									●

Seabirds breeding on principal islands in central Pacific Ocean, **south of the Equator.** *Note*: other non-breeding species not quoted but may be seen locally in the vicinity.

	Marquesas Is	Tuamotu Arch	Pitcairn Group	Society Is	Austral Is	Phoenix Is	Cook Is	Samoan Is	Tonga Is	Fiji Arch	Ellice Is	New Hebrides	Bismarck Arch	Solomon Is	New Caledonia Is
Tahiti Petrel	●	–	–	●	–	–	–	–	–	–	–	–	–		●
Phoenix Petrel	●	●	●	–	–	●	–	–	●	–	–	–	–	–	–
Herald Petrel	●	●	●	–	–	–	–	–	●	–	–	–	–	–	–
Bulwer's Petrel	●	–	–	–	–	●	–	–	–	–	–	–	–	–	–
Wedge-tailed Shearwater	●	●	●	●	●	●	–	●	●	●	–	●	–	●	●
Christmas Shearwater	●	●	●	–	●	●	–	–	–	–	–	–	–	–	–
Audubon's Shearwater	●	●	–	●	–	●	–	–	–	●	–	●	–	–	●
White-throated Storm-petrel	●	–	–	–	–	●	–	●	–	●	–	●	–	–	–
White-tailed Tropic-bird	●	●	–	●	●	●	–	●	●	●	●	–	–	–	●
Brown Booby	●	●	–	●	●	●	–	–	●	●	–	–	–	–	●
Red-footed Booby	●	●	●	●	●	●	–	●	–	●	–	–	–	–	–
Great Frigate-bird	●	●	●	●	–	●	–	–	–	–	–	–	–	–	●
Lesser Frigate-bird	●	●	–	●	–	●	●	–	●	●	–	–	–	–	●
Sooty Tern	●	●	●	●	●	●	–	●	●	●	●	–	●	–	●
Blue-grey Noddy	●	●	●	●	–	●	–	●	●	●	–	●	–	–	●
Brown Noddy	●	●	●	●	●	●	●	●	●	●	●	●	●	●	●
White-capped Noddy	●	●	–	●	–	●	–	●	●	●	●	●	●	–	●
White Tern	●	●	●	●	●	●	●	●	●	●	●	●	–	●	●
Murphy's Petrel	–	●	●	–	●	–	–	–	–	–	–	–	–	–	–
Kermadec Petrel	–	●	●	–	●	–	–	–	–	–	–	–	–	–	–
Red-tailed Tropic-bird	–	●	●	●	●	●	●	●	●	●	–	●	–	–	●
Blue-faced Booby	–	●	●	–	–	●	–	●	–	●	–	–	–	–	–
Spectacled Tern	–	●	–	–	–	●	–	●	–	●	–	–	–	●	–
Crested Tern	–	●	–	●	–	–	–	–	●	●	●	●	●	–	●
Collared Petrel	–	–	–	●	–	●	–	–	–	●	–	●	–	–	●
White-bellied Storm-petrel	–	–	–	–	–	–	–	–	–	–	–	–	–	–	–
Black-naped Tern	–	–	–	–	–	–	–	●	–	●	●	●	●	●	●
Little Pied Cormorant	–	–	–	–	–	–	–	–	–	●	–	●	–	●	●
Roseate Tern	–	–	–	–	–	–	–	–	–	–	–	●	–	●	●
Bridled Tern	–	–	–	–	–	–	–	–	–	–	–	–	●	●	–
Silver Gull	–	–	–	–	–	–	–	–	–	–	–	–	–	–	●

Index

References are to route numbers. A = Antarctica

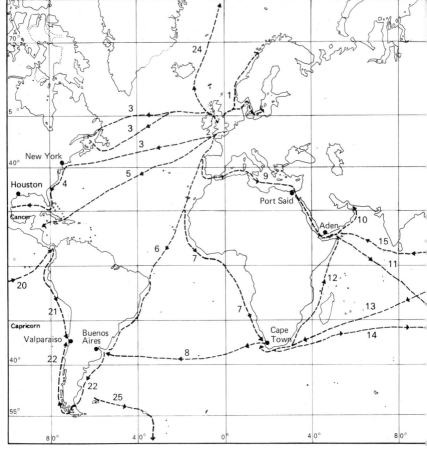

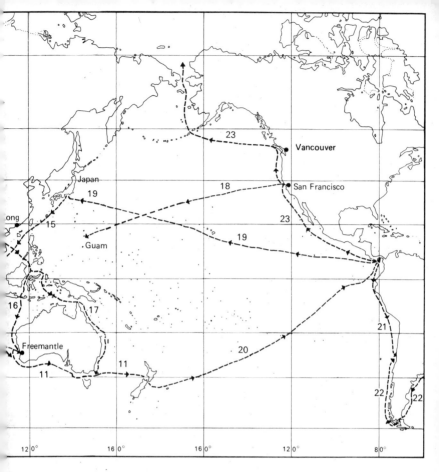